CherryPy Essentials

Rapid Python Web Application Development

Design, develop, test, and deploy your Python
web applications easily

Sylvain Hellegouarch

BIRMINGHAM - MUMBAI

CherryPy Essentials
Rapid Python Web Application Development

First published: March 2007

Production Reference: 2220307

Published by Packt Publishing Ltd.
32 Lincoln Road
Olton
Birmingham, B27 6PA, UK.

ISBN 978-1-904811-84-8

www.packtpub.com

Cover Image by www.visionwt.com

Credits

Author

Sylvain Hellegouarch

Reviewers

Rémi Delon

Robert Brewer

Development Editor

Nanda Padmanabhan

Technical Editors

Saurabh Singh

Shayantani Chaudhuri

Ved Prakash Jha

Editorial Manager

Dipali Chittar

Project Manager

Patricia Weir

Project Coordinator

Sagara Naik

Indexer

Bhushan Pangaonkar

Proofreader

Chris Smith

Layouts and Illustrations

Shantanu Zagade

Manjiri Nadkarni

Cover Designer

Shantanu Zagade

About the Author

Sylvain Hellegouarch is an IT Software Consultant dedicated to the development of free software projects such as CherryPy. Since 2004, he has been coordinating and administrating the community efforts around the project providing support for newcomers and seasoned developers, alike. In 2006, he developed 'bridge' and 'amplee', two Python-based projects centered on XML and the upcoming Atom Publishing Protocol respectively.

He has also been deeply involved in The Viberavetions Project, a comprehensive grassroots solution for independent artists and musicians to better connect with consumers, as well as the nuXleus project, a platform designed for faster, more reliable inter- and intra-application and personal communication.

Born in France, Sylvain graduated with a degree in Computer Science from South Brittany University, Lorient, France in 2002. Since then he has been working as an IT consultant for a variety of companies, both small and large. He currently resides in the United Kingdom.

Acknowledgement

Throwing myself into the adventure of writing a book was a challenge I had in mind for a while before Packt Publishing came along and I do thank them for trusting me on the CherryPy book. Overall writing a book is a task you can't carry alone; editors and reviewers are critical to the release of a good quality book. I thoroughly thank Robert Brewer and Rémi Delon for undertaking the task of reviewing my work and I much appreciate how difficult it has been. Both contributed complementary feedback that hopefully will make you enjoy reading this book. Beyond that I want to thank Robert for making CherryPy such a fantastic product to use; I hope this book will show how professional CherryPy is. Of course all of this would not have been possible if Rémi, the founder of the project, had not given the keys and his full trust to the community for carrying the project. In addition I would like to thank Christian Wyglendowski who has done a fantastic job at supporting the community for so long with such indulgence and sense of humor. I would also like to give thanks to my contacts at Packt Publishing, Nanda Padmanabhan, Patricia Weir, and Suneet Amrute for their support and patience throughout the making of this book. They have trusted me and listened to my concerns in a way that I can only be grateful for.

I also want to acknowledge the support I received from folks at the Viberavetions project especially M. David Peterson who has become a close friend, without forgetting Uche Ogbuji, Russ Miles and Kurt Cagle who have all shared their views at times when I needed them.

I heartily want to thank all my friends who have always respected my passion for being part of open-source projects and communities while reminding me that there is more to life than lines of code. They have been a breath of fresh air to me throughout these years and a great comfort when times weren't good: one person particularly who has taken a great place in my life and who has always pushed me ahead.

Lastly I want to deeply thank my beloved family for always being discreetly there for me and supporting my decisions even when they did not look like they were in my best interests. You have never failed me and the work I have put into this book is a way for me to thank you for that. Merci à vous.

This book is for the CherryPy community and beyond.

About the Reviewers

Rémi Delon is a French software developer and entrepreneur living in London, UK. He has been developing software for over 10 years and contributing to the open-source community for over five years. He is the original creator of CherryPy and is now running WebFaction, a fast growing hosting service specialized in agile tools, including CherryPy and TurboGears.

Robert Brewer is the System Architect for Amor Ministries, a non-profit house-building ministry that serves the poors of Mexico.

He is the lead developer of the CherryPy project, and wrote most of version 3.0. He is also the author of the modpython gateway for WSGI, and is the creator of Dejavu, a pure-Python Object-Relational Mapper.

Founded in 2003 by the original CherryPy creator, WebFaction is a reliable and affordable hosting provider for your CherryPy applications.

You can get an exclusive 20% discount by using the promo code "CHERRYPYBOOK" when you sign up with WebFaction, visit http://www.webfaction.com for more details.

Table of Contents

Preface

Over the last few years, the boom that the World has experienced with the Internet breakthrough has pushed almost every programming language or platform to welcome the rise of web development toolkits, libraries, and frameworks.

The Python programming language has grown a rather large list of these environments though apart from a few of them such as Zope and Twisted most have a fairly small community. It is in this context that CherryPy came into existence when Rémi Delon, its creator, decided that he needed a tool that would work as he wanted for his own personal projects. He then released CherryPy under a free software license so that anyone could use, distribute, and contribute to the project.

CherryPy is a Python library implementing the HTTP protocol, which is at the very core of the Web, using common Python idioms. On top of that CherryPy offers its own view and concepts on how to help a developer to build web applications while being minimally intrusive through its own simple and straightforward API.

This book will guide you through the CherryPy library with the aim of giving you the key to make the best of it in your own web applications.

The first four chapters are dedicated to CherryPy, providing information ranging from its history to an in-depth presentation of its key features. The rest of the book will then take you into the development of a photoblog application. Each chapter tries to provide enough background to allow you to ponder the why and how of each decision made. Indeed writing software applications is not a precise science and compromises need to be undertaken for the better, however, the truth is that writing software usually does not go quite as planned. I have written this book with the hope that in the end you would have learnt much more than using a Python library.

What This Book Covers

Chapter 1 presents the story behind CherryPy and a high-level overview of the project.

Chapter 2 guides you through the installation and deployment of CherryPy via common strategies like using distutils, setuptools, or subversion.

Chapter 3 gives an overview of the main and the most common aspects of CherryPy, which will give you an understanding of what the library can do.

Chapter 4 goes into an in-depth review of the main aspects of the library such as its support for the HTTP protocol or the WSGI interface. It also extensively discusses the tool feature of the CherryPy API.

Chapter 5 introduces the application, which will be the unifying theme for the rest of the book. The chapter reviews the basic entities that the application will manipulate before moving onto explaining how we will map them into a relational database. This will allow us to explain the concept of ORM and perform a quick comparison between SQLAlchemy, SQLObject, and Dejavu.

Chapter 6 presents the idea behind web services by reviewing REST and the Atom Publishing Protocol.

Chapter 7 describes how to use a templating engine such as Kid to generate web pages dynamically. The chapter also introduces Mochikit a JavaScript toolkit to perform client-side development.

Chapter 8 extends chapter 7 by diving into the world of Ajax, which has reminded web developers that they can create extremely powerful applications by simply using the browser capabilities, the JavaScript language, and the HTTP protocol.

Chapter 9 makes a strong point that any application should be reasonably well tested and introduces some testing strategies like unit testing, functional testing, and load testing.

Chapter 10 ends the book by reviewing some methods to deploy a CherryPy application under a common web-server front end like Apache and lighttpd. The chapter also explains how to enable SSL from your CherryPy application.

What You Need for This Book

Throughout this book we will assume that you have the following packages installed and available.

- Python 2.4 or above
- CherryPy 3.0

You need to have a basic knowledge of the Python language.

Who is This Book for

The book is principally geared towards web developers who wish to learn how the Python programming language can fit their requirements. Although the CherryPy toolkit is at the core of the book, many common libraries are introduced in order to open the book to a larger audience.

Conventions

In this book, you will find a number of styles of text that distinguish between different kinds of information. Here are some examples of these styles, and an explanation of their meaning.

There are three styles for code. Code words in text are shown as follows: "A newer and more common way of deploying a package is to use the `easy_install` command to install eggs."

A block of code will be set as follows:

```
body
{
  background-color: #663;
  color: #fff;
}
p
{
  text-align: center;
}
```

Any command-line input and output is written as follows:

```
python ez_setup.py
```

New terms and **important words** are introduced in a bold-type font. Words that you see on the screen, in menus or dialog boxes for example, appear in our text like this: "The next step is to run those tests by clicking the **All** button."

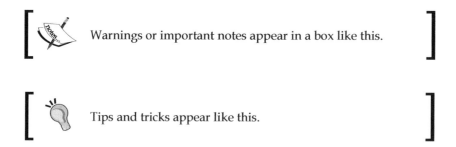

Warnings or important notes appear in a box like this.

Tips and tricks appear like this.

Reader Feedback

Feedback from our readers is always welcome. Let us know what you think about this book, what you liked or may have disliked. Reader feedback is important for us to develop titles that you really get the most out of.

To send us general feedback, simply drop an email to feedback@packtpub.com, making sure to mention the book title in the subject of your message.

If there is a book that you need and would like to see us publish, please send us a note in the **SUGGEST A TITLE** form on www.packtpub.com or email suggest@ packtpub.com.

If there is a topic that you have expertise in and you are interested in either writing or contributing to a book, see our author guide on www.packtpub.com/authors.

Customer Support

Now that you are the proud owner of a Packt book, we have a number of things to help you to get the most from your purchase.

Downloading the Example Code for the Book

Visit http://www.packtpub.com/support, and select this book from the list of titles to download any example code or extra resources for this book. The files available for download will then be displayed.

The downloadable files contain instructions on how to use them.

Errata

Although we have taken every care to ensure the accuracy of our contents, mistakes do happen. If you find a mistake in one of our books—maybe a mistake in text or code—we would be grateful if you would report this to us. By doing this you can save other readers from frustration, and help to improve subsequent versions of this book. If you find any errata, report them by visiting http://www.packtpub.com/support, selecting your book, clicking on the **Submit Errata** link, and entering the details of your errata. Once your errata are verified, your submission will be accepted and the errata are added to the list of existing errata. The existing errata can be viewed by selecting your title from http://www.packtpub.com/support.

Questions

You can contact us at questions@packtpub.com if you are having a problem with some aspect of the book, and we will do our best to address it.

Introduction to CherryPy

1

The use of the World Wide Web has grown exponentially, and has become a key component of the way we live today. From the developer's point of view, the Web offers great opportunities and good fun. However, the growing number of technologies oriented towards the Web is overwhelming, and it can be difficult to decide which one to use. The goal of this book is to present one of these, CherryPy, a Python web-application library.

This chapter will introduce CherryPy's features and strengths, beginning with a summary of CherryPy's history, then looking at its friendly community, which has long been an important piece of the project's success, and finally reviewing key principles behind the evolution of CherryPy.

Overview

CherryPy is a Python library providing a friendly interface to the HTTP protocol for Python developers. HTTP is the backbone of the World Wide Web. Web applications have grown exponentially in the last few years. This explosion was followed by a large number of toolkits, libraries, and frameworks released in various programming languages to help web developers in their task. Ultimately all of these aim at making a web developer's life much easier. In this context CherryPy has started using Python's strengths as a dynamic language to model and bind the HTTP protocol into a API that follows Python idioms.

The Python community has grown a large number of web libraries and frameworks over the years to the point where it has become some kind of a joke as much as a worry. Even though only a handful of them have attracted most of the community, (TurboGears, Django, or Zope) each existing library or framework has kept its niche influence by providing its own view on how to interface Python with HTTP and the Web in general. CherryPy was born because at that time Remi Delon, its creator, could not find what he wanted in the existing choices. Over the years, the design of

CherryPy has been tuned by new developers who liked its strengths and joined in. Today the project has a strong community base that uses it on a daily basis in many different contexts.

History of CherryPy

Remi Delon released the first version of CherryPy in late June 2002. This was the starting point of a successful Python web library. Remi is a French hacker who has trusted Python for being ultimately one of the greatest alternatives for web application development.

The project attracted a number of developers who were interested in the approach taken by Remi:

- CherryPy classes were an extension to Python to support the separation of concern between the data and the presentation. It was close to the model-view-controller pattern.
- A CherryPy class has to be processed and compiled by the CherryPy engine to produce a self-contained Python module embedding the complete application as well as its own built-in web server.

CherryPy would map a URL and its query string into a Python method call, for example: `http://somehost.net/echo?message=hello` would map to `echo(message='hello')`.

During the following two years, the project was supported by the community and Remi released several improved versions.

In June 2004, a discussion started about the future of the project and whether it should continue with the same architecture. One of the main concerns was the compilation step, which did not feel natural to Python developers. Brainstorming and discussion by several project regulars then led to the concept of object-publishing engine and filters, which soon became a core ingredient of CherryPy 2.

Eventually, in October 2004, the first version of CherryPy 2 alpha was released as a proof of concept of these core ideas. Then followed six months of intense work to release a stable version (late April 2005). Soon other developers joined the project to improve it. CherryPy 2.0 was a real success; however, it was recognized that its design could still be improved, and needed refactoring.

After further community feedback/discussions, CherryPy's API was further modified to improve its elegance, leading to the release of CherryPy 2.1.0 in October 2005. This version was shipped by the popular TurboGears project—itself a stack of projects to produce a web mega-framework. The team released CherryPy 2.2.0 in April 2006.

CherryPy's presence as a core ingredient in the increasingly widely adopted TurboGears stack naturally meant that more and more issues were raised about some aspects of CherryPy. For example, its WSGI support, the lack of up-to-date documentation, or its only-average performance. It was clear that to meet these real and important requirements, it would be extremely difficult to extend CherryPy 2 without breaking backward-compatibility constraints. As a result, the decision was finally made to move towards CherryPy 3, which was released at the end of 2006.

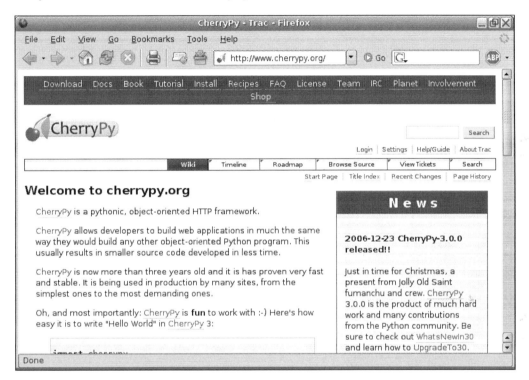

The Community

CherryPy would not be where it stands without the community built over the last few years. Remi has always been clear about the fact that he does not want CherryPy to be his pet project, but rather to be a community one.

CherryPy has always had its followers, but the CherryPy community actually started with version 2.0 of the product. In November 2004, an IRC channel was registered on the **Open** and **Free Technology Community (OFTC)** network to allow developers and users to quickly exchange ideas or to report defects. The channel gradually attracted more and more regulars and was generally recognized to be a very friendly place. In addition to the IRC channel, mailing-lists were created for developers and users. Eventually a feed aggregation of blog entries of regular CherryPy users was published and has been available since then at `http://planet.cherrypy.org`.

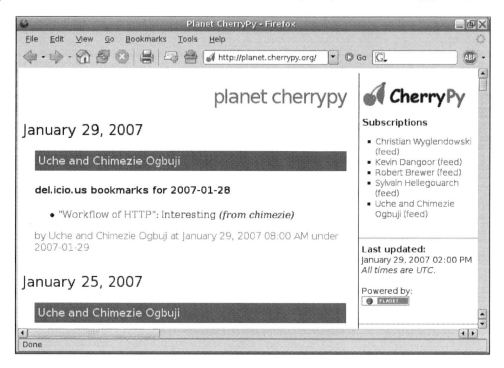

CherryPy Project Strengths

- Simplicity: One of the main goals has always been to keep CherryPy as simple as possible with the aim of avoiding the library to over engineering the project. Thanks to the narrow scope covered by the library, the developers have been able to concentrate on the API and community feedback.

- Self-contained: From the very beginning, Remi decided that the core of CherryPy would not require any third-party Python packages to work and would rely purely on the Python standard library.

- Not intrusive: Another critical aspect of the library the developers have long cared about was to make sure that CherryPy would stay as much as possible out of the way of its users. The idea was to provide a set of tools to any developer making no assumptions about the way in which he or she may choose to use them.

- Open to discussion: The developer team has always listened to the feedback given by the community. This does not mean that every request has been adopted, but almost all have been discussed and reviewed.

- Fun: When working on an open-source project, contributors should not be made to feel it is just their day-to-day job; on the contrary there is great value in them really enjoying what they do. Likewise, for a CherryPy user, the fun element is also an important part, and we observe that it makes each of us better and more creative developers.

Beyond CherryPy

In its early days, CherryPy attracted a small group of users but its design prevented it from growing into something larger or from being used more widely. Moreover, at that time the Python web-development field was mainly occupied by the Zope platform. When CherryPy 2 was released, its conception was more warmly welcomed by the community and eventually attracted more users who started to use it for applications as well as for building their own packages based on top of it.

Indeed in late September 2005, Kevin Dangoor released TurboGears—a framework for web development built as a stack of existing open-source products. Kevin chose CherryPy to handle the HTTP layer of his framework, SQLObject to map objects to the database, Kid for XHTML templating, and MochiKit for client-side handling. This release took place just a couple of months after another Python web framework, Django, was opened to the community. Both projects quickly gained a lot of popularity among the Python community and thanks to a little competition between them, they grew in a very quick fashion. The boom of TurboGears boosted CherryPy's fame and attracted an important volume of new users.

These waves of new developers increased CherryPy's number of requested features as well as defects being fixed, leading eventually to CherryPy 3, the most stable version of the library, and to the writing of this book.

CherryPy's future is clear and bright; the fantastic work done by Robert Brewer has allowed the library to reach its cruising speed. TurboGears' future version will certainly move to CherryPy 3, which will lead to a whole new set of questions to be brought up to the development team and will push CherryPy to its next big step.

Through the Book

This book aims at introducing the CherryPy library at a level that should make you confident that you can use it best in your own web application. Additionally we will try to open the discussion on the design of web applications and a perspective of the domain at the time of writing the book. In a nutshell the book will explain how to get and install CherryPy in a number of common ways in the Python community, such as using setup tools and easy_install. It will also give an overview of the main and most common aspects of CherryPy. This will gently bring you into an understanding of what the library can do. It then drills down into the library features such as its HTTP capabilities, alternative URI dispatchers, and extending the library as well as its WSGI support.

This will give you a solid understanding of CherryPy, its design, and how to make the best use of it from within your own applications. The book then breaks down the layers of web development by introducing techniques and tools such as object-relational mappers, web services, and Ajax through the development of a simple blog application.

It presents the blog application objectives and boundaries, reviews the status of database handling in Python, and then explains Object-Relational Mapping. It extensively presents one of the Python ORMs called Dejavu. It also talks about REST and the Atom Publishing Protocol, both of which offer a way to design web services that can extend your web applications beyond the simple capacity of serving HTML pages. Then it introduces you to the presentation layer of the blog application, which encompasses the review of the templating engine called Kid as well as the JavaScript library called MochiKit. The book discusses Ajax and how your applications can benefit from the principles behind it. We will also see how your application can call the web services. Then, the book extensively inspects the field of testing a web application. This goes from unit testing to load testing via the functional testing aspect of it. The book finally ends by presenting different ways to deploy a web application as a stand-alone application or via well known web servers such as Apache and lighttpd.

Although some chapters do not extensively include discussion about CherryPy itself, all of them will converge towards bringing an understanding of some aspects of web application development. Hopefully this book will teach you about CherryPy and will also give you the knowledge and the desire to learn more about the topics it covers

Summary

After reading this introduction you should have the necessary background understanding of where this book is going to lead you. CherryPy is a simple and yet powerful Python library that will be a great companion to web developers who wish to find a package that hides the difficulties of the HTTP protocol while keeping its strengths. The CherryPy community has been working hard for the last few years to make such a product possible; hopefully this book will give you the right directions to make the most of it.

2
Download and
Install CherryPy

Like most open-source projects, CherryPy can be downloaded and installed in various ways. Here we will discuss the following three methods:

- Using a tarball
- Using easy_install
- Getting the latest version of the source code using Subversion

Each one brings a different value to the users of the project and it is important to understand the contribution made by each.

Once you have read this chapter, you should be able to retrieve and deploy CherryPy, as well as understand how to use each technique for your own software.

Requirements

Throughout this book we will assume you have the following packages installed and available.

- Python 2.4 or above
- CherryPy 3.0

We will also assume you have knowledge of Python itself as we will not cover the language.

Overview

Installing a Python module or package is usually an easy process. First let's discuss the most common way to build and install a new package, thanks to a standard module, distutils, which appeared with Python 2.0.

This module provides a clean interface for specifying how a package is structured, what are the required dependencies, and the building rules of the package. For the user, it usually means typing the following commands:

```
python setup.py build
python setup.py install
```

The first one will simply build the package against the rules defined by the developers, reporting errors so that the end user knows about a missing dependency for example. The second one will install the package in the default directory used by Python to store third-party packages or modules. Note that the latter command will call the former by default to quickly check that nothing has changed since the last run.

The default directories where packages and modules are stored are:

- On UNIX or Linux
  `/usr/local/lib/python2.4/site-packages` or
  `/usr/lib/python2.4/site-packages`
- On Microsoft Windows
  `C:\Python or C:\Python2x`
- On MacOS
  `Python:Lib:site-packages`

On UNIX or Linux it will depend how your Python installation has been deployed, but the directories given above are the most common. When importing a module, Python will look into a list of directories, some defaults and others provided by the user, until it finds a matching module or else an exception will be raised. The searched list can be modified either by defining the PYTHONPATH environment variable or by amending it from the code itself as follows:

```
import sys
sys.path.append(path)
```

The PYTHONPATH environment variable is one of the variables read by the Python engine when it is being launched. It contains additional paths to append to the searched list of paths for third-party modules and packages.

Another method is to set a file named after the package with the .pth extension. This file should contain the full path of the package.

Notwithstanding its simplicity, this algorithm has its limitations. Since the sys.path list is ordered you have to make sure that if two paths contain the same module with different versions, the one your application imports is the first one to be reached. This leads us to the following package versioning problem.

Imagine that you install CherryPy 2.2.1 in your global installation of Python; it would be available under the directory /usr/local/lib/site-packages/ cherrypy. However, the path does not contain the version information of the package. Therefore, if you must install CherryPy 3.0.0 as well, you have to overwrite the existing installation.

Luckily the Python community has come up with a solution to this problem—eggs. An **egg** is a compressed folder containing all the files and sub-folders of a package with the version details of the package in its name.

An egg is a distributable bundle, by default zipped, of a Python package or module including information such as the author and the version of the package.

For example, CherryPy 2.2.1 built by Python 2.4 would look like the following: Cherrypy-2.2.1-py2.4.egg. An egg by itself is not very useful; its deployment requires easy_install, a Python module that contains the logic for handling eggs. This means you can have multiple versions deployed in the same directory and leave it up to easy_install to decide which one to load.

In the next sections we will see in detail how to install CherryPy using the most common cases.

Installation from a Tarball

A **tarball** is a compressed archive of a file or directory. The name comes from the use of the tar utility found on UNIX and related operating systems.

 Historically the compression used has usually been `gzip` and the extension of a *tarball* is either `.tar.gz` or `.tgz`.

CherryPy provides a tarball for each release whether it is alpha, beta, release candidate, or stable. They can all be retrieved from `http://download.cherrypy.org/`.

CherryPy tarballs contain the complete source code of the library.

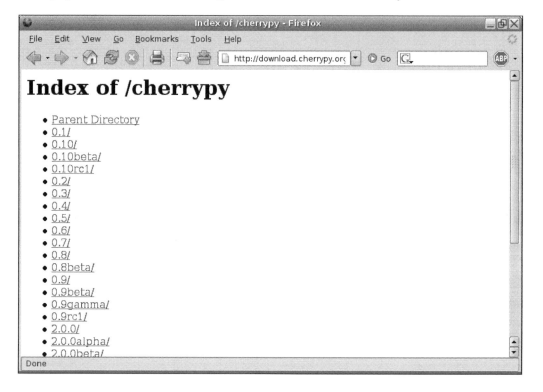

To install CherryPy from a tarball you need to go through the following steps:

1. Download the version that interests you from
   `http://download.cherrypy.org/`.

2. Go to the directory where the tarball has been downloaded and uncompress it:

   ° If you are using Linux, type the following command:

   ```
   tar zxvf cherrypy-x.y.z.tgz
   ```

   In the given command, `x.y.z` is the version you have fetched.

   ° If you are running Microsoft Windows, you can use a utility such as 7-Zip to uncompress the archive via a graphical interface.

3. Move to the newly created directory and enter the following command, which will build CherryPy:

   ```
   python setup.py build
   ```

4. Finally, in order to do a global installation you have to issue the following command (you will more than likely need administrator permissions):

   ```
   python setup.py install
   ```

 Note that these commands will have to be issued from a command line. Under Microsoft Windows you will run those from a DOS command prompt

The above steps will perform a global installation of CherryPy on your system for the default Python environment. There are cases where this is not suitable or not possible. For example, you may want to install CherryPy only for a given version of Python; in that case you will have to specify the correct Python binary such as `python2.4` in steps 3 and 4 mentioned earlier.

It may also happen that you prefer not to do a global installation, in that case the quickest way under UNIX and Linux is to replace step 4 mentioned earlier with:

```
python setup.py install --home=~
```

This will put the files in `$HOME/lib/python` where `$HOME` represents your home directory.

Under Microsoft Windows, which has no knowledge of HOME, you would do the following:

```
python setup.py install --prefix=c:\some\path
```

The path you choose is not important in itself and you can use whatever suits your environment.

Then you will have to make sure Python goes through that directory when you need to import modules. The easiest way is to set the PYTHONPATH environment variable to the following:

- On Linux using a bash shell

```
export PYTHONPATH=~/lib/python
```

- On Microsoft Windows using a command prompt

```
set PYTHONPATH=/some/path/
```

> Note that this will only last while the Command window is opened and will be dropped once you close it. To make the changes permanent you should set the global PYTHONPATH variable via **System Properties | Advanced | Environment Variables**.

- On MacOS using a csh shell

```
setenv PYTHONPATH "/some/path/"
```

The PYTHONPATH environment variable will be read at startup by the Python interpreter, which will append it to its internal system path.

Installation through Easy Install

Easy_install is a Python module that can be found on the **Python Enterprise Application Kit (PEAK)** website to facilitate the deployment of Python packages and modules. From the developer's point of view, it provides an easy API to import Python modules either for a given version or a range of versions. For instance, here is what you would do to load the first CherryPy version greater than 2.2 found in your environment:

```
>>> from pkg_resources import require
>>> require("cherrypy>=2.2")
[CherryPy 2.2.1 (/home/sylvain/lib/python/
CherryPy-2.2.1-py2.4.egg)]
```

From the user's point of view it simplifies the procedure of downloading, building, and deploying Python products.

Before installing CherryPy, we must install easy_install itself. Download the
`ez_setup.py` module from `http://peak.telecommunity.com/dist/ez_setup.py`
and run it as follows, as a user with administrative rights on the computer:

python ez_setup.py

If you do not have administrator permission, you can use the `-install-dir (-d)`
option as follows:

python ez_setup.py -install-dir=/some/path

Make sure that `/some/path` is part of the Python system path. You can set
`PYTHONPATH` to that directory for example.

This will set up your environment to support easy_install. Then to install a Python
product that supports easy_install, you should issue the following command:

easy_install product_name

easy_install will search the **Python Package Index (PyPI)** to find the given product.
PyPI is a centralized repository of information about Python products.

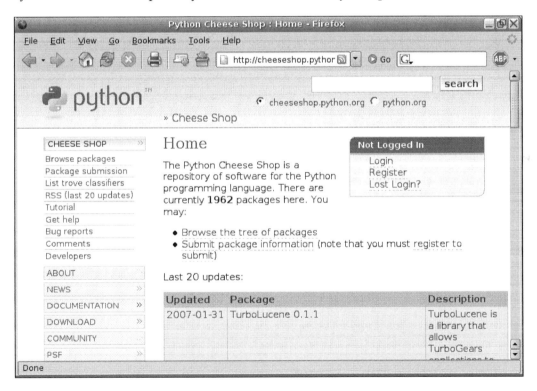

In order to deploy the latest available version of CherryPy, you should then issue the following command:

```
easy_install cherrypy
```

easy_install will then download CherryPy, build, and install it globally to your Python environment. If you prefer installing it in a specific location, you will have to enter the following command:

```
easy_install --install-dir=~ cherrypy
```

Once installed, you will have a file named `cherrypy.x.y.z-py2.4.egg` depending on the latest version of CherryPy.

Installation from Subversion

Subversion is an excellent open-source revision control system that allows developers to carry out projects in a controlled and concurrent manner.

The basic principle of such systems is to register a resource and then keep track of every change made to it, so that any developer can retrieve any previous version, compare two versions, or even follow the evolution over time of the said resource. A resource can be a source code file, a binary, an image, documentation, or anything that is expressible in machine-readable form.

Subversion is centralized, so a project is managed by a subversion server and each client has a copy of it. The developer works on that copy and commits back any changes he or she has made. When a conflict arises, for instance, if another developer has modified the same file and has committed it already, the server will let you know and forbid your commit until you resolve the issue.

Subversion is atomic, which means that if a commit fails on one file the whole commit fails. On the other hand if it succeeds the entire project revision is incremented, not just the files involved.

Subversion is often viewed as the successor of CVS and is considered much friendlier. However, other revision systems also exist such as Monotone or Darcs.

Under Linux, you can either install Subversion from its sources or using a package manager. Let's describe the procedure for the source code.

1. Get the latest tarball from `http://subversion.tigris.org/`

2. Then type the following command in the command console:

   `tar zxvf subversion-x.y.z.tar.gz`

3. Enter the newly created directory and type: `./configure`

4. Then to build the package itself type: `make`

5. You might later need the Python binding for Subversion as well:
   `make swig-py`

6. To install Subversion globally, you will need to be the administrator and then enter: `make install; make install-swig-py`

Most of the time, under Linux or UNIX, it is easier to use Subversion through the command line. However, if you prefer to use a graphical interface, I would advise you to install a fat client application such as eSvn or kdesvn.

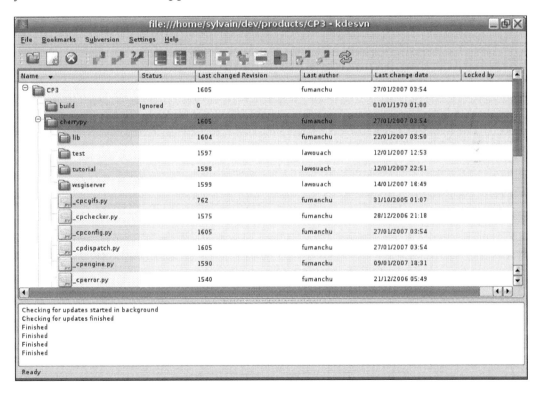

Under Microsoft Windows, it is much easier to directly use a graphical application such as TortoiseSVN, which will install the Subversion client as well.

Getting CherryPy using Subversion is recommended in the following situations:

- A feature exists or a bug has been fixed and is only available in code under development.
- You decide to work on CherryPy itself.
- You need to branch from the main trunk in order to *try and see* a feature, a new design, or simply backport bug fixing in a previous release.

In order to use the most recent version of the project, you will first need to check out the trunk folder found on the Subversion repository. Enter the following command from a shell:

```
svn co http://svn.cherrypy.org/trunk cherrypy
```

 Under Microsoft Windows you can do this from a command line or simply use TortoiseSVN. Please refer to its documentation for more information.

This will create a `cherrypy` directory and download the complete source code into it. As it is usually not recommended to deploy globally a version under development; you would type the following command to install CherryPy into a local directory:

- Under Linux and related systems using a console:

```
python setup.py install --home=~
```

- Under Microsoft Windows using the command prompt:

```
python setup.py install --prefix=c:\some\path
```

Then simply point the PYTHONPATH environment variable to the chosen directory.

Note that this directory does not matter as long as it is reachable by the Python process via PYTHONPATH or the standard sys module.

Testing your Installation

Whichever way you decide to install and deploy CherryPy in your environment, you must be able to import it from the Python shell as follows:

```
>>> import cherrypy
>>> cherrypy.__version__
'3.0.0'
```

If you do not install CherryPy globally to your Python environment, do not forget to set the PYTHONPATH environment variable, else you will get an error as follows:

```
>>> import cherrypy
Traceback (most recent call last):
  File "<stdin>", line 1, in ?
ImportError: No module named cherrypy
```

Keeping CherryPy Up to Date

Updating or upgrading CherryPy will depend on the approach you have taken to install it.

- Installed using a tarball

  Usually the cleanest way to ensure the update goes smoothly is to first remove the directory containing the package from its location in sys.path, then to follow the steps described previously to install the library.

- Installed using easy_install

  Updating is one of the key features provided by easy_install.

  ```
  easy_install -U cherrypy
  ```

  As the eggs containing the library are named after the version they serve, you can simply follow the steps defined in the previous section without removing an existing egg. Be careful though, as this only holds true when the application running specifies precisely which version it requires.

- Installed using Subversion

  The interesting aspect of this approach is that you can update the library almost continuously. To update your installation, you need to enter svn update from the top directory holding the source code and then issue the python setup.py install command.

 As always remember to take a backup of your files before doing an update.

Summary

We have discussed in this chapter the different ways of installing CherryPy in your environment via three techniques. The traditional approach is to use an archive containing all the files of the Python package to install and use the `setup.py` module within that archive. A newer and more common way of deploying a package is to use the `easy_install` command to install eggs. Finally, if you wish to be synchronized with the latest development of CherryPy, you can get the package from its Subversion repository. Whichever method you follow, they will all lead to CherryPy being available on your system.

3

Overview of CherryPy

In the first chapter we briefly reviewed some aspects of CherryPy; it is now time to dig deeper and see how the project is designed and structured. We will first go through a basic CherryPy example. Then we will go through the CherryPy core, the publishing-object engine, and see how it wraps the HTTP protocol in an object-oriented library. Our next step will be to explore the concept of hooking into the core, the CherryPy library, and the tool mechanism. We will then review how CherryPy handles errors and exceptions and how you can benefit from it.

By the end of this chapter you will have a good overview of the CherryPy library; however, it is likely you will need to come back to this chapter during the rest of the book in order to fully appreciate it.

Vocabulary

In order to avoid misunderstandings, we need to define a few key words that will be used throughout this book.

Keyword	Definition
Web server	A web server is the interface dealing with the HTTP protocol. Its goal is to transform incoming HTTP requests into entities that are then passed to the application server and also transform information from the application server back into HTTP responses.
Application	An application is a piece of software that takes a unit of information, applies business logic to it, and returns a processed unit of information.
Application server	An application server is the component hosting one or more applications.
Web application server	A web application server is simply the aggregation of a web server and an application server into a single component.

CherryPy is a web application server.

Basic Example

To illustrate the CherryPy library we will go through a very basic web application allowing a user to leave a note on the main page through an HTML form. The notes will be stacked and be rendered in a reverse order of their creation date. We will use a session object to store the name of the author of the note.

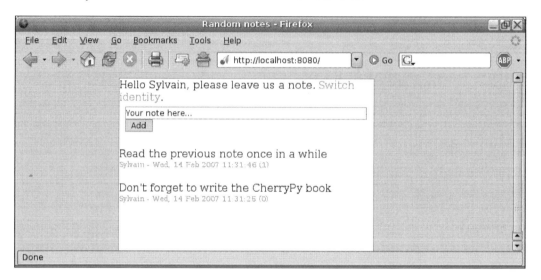

Each note will have a URI attached to itself, of the form /note/id.

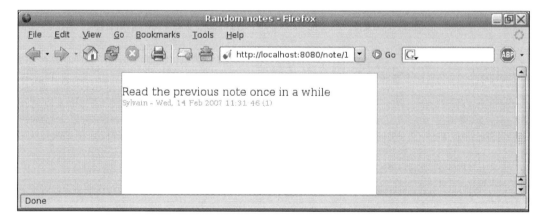

Create a blank file named note.py and copy the following source code.

```
#!/usr/bin/python
# -*- coding: utf-8 -*

# Python standard library imports
```

```
import os.path
import time
###############################################################
#The unique module to be imported to use cherrypy
###############################################################
import cherrypy

# CherryPy needs an absolute path when dealing with static data
_curdir = os.path.join(os.getcwd(), os.path.dirname(__file__))

###############################################################
# We will keep our notes into a global list
# Please not that it is hazardous to use a simple list here
# since we will run the application in a multi-threaded environment
# which will not protect the access to this list
# In a more realistic application we would need either to use a
# thread safe object or to manually protect from concurrent access
# to this list
###############################################################
_notes = []

###############################################################
# A few HTML templates
###############################################################
_header = """
<html>
  <head>
    <title>Random notes</<title>
    <link rel="stylesheet" type="text/css" href="/style.css"></link>
  </head>
  <body>
  <div class="container">"""

_footer = """
  </div>
  </body>
</html>"""

_note_form = """
  <div class="form">
  <form method="post" action="post" class="form">
    <input type="text" value="Your note here..." name="text"
           size="60"></input>
    <input type="submit" value="Add"></input>
  </form>
  </div>"""

_author_form = """
```

```
    <div class="form">
    <form method="post" action="set">
      <input type="text" name="name"></input>
      <input type="submit" value="Switch"></input>
    </form>
    </div>"""

_note_view = """
<br />
<div>
    %s
    <div class="info">%s - %s <a href="/note/%d">(%d)</a></div>
</div>"""


####################################################################
# Our only domain object (sometimes referred as to a Model)
####################################################################
class Note(object):
    def __init__(self, author, note):
        self.id = None
        self.author = author
        self.note = note
        self.timestamp = time.gmtime(time.time())

    def __str__(self):
        return self.note


####################################################################
# The main entry point of the Note application
####################################################################
class NoteApp:
    """
    The base application which will be hosted by CherryPy
    """
    # Here we tell CherryPy we will enable the session
    # from this level of the tree of published objects
    # as well as its sub-levels
    _cp_config = { 'tools.sessions.on': True }

    def _render_note(self, note):
        """Helper to render a note into HTML"""
        return _note_view % (note, note.author,
                              time.strftime("%a, %d %b %Y %H:%M:%S",
                                            note.timestamp),
                              note.id, note.id)
```

```
@cherrypy.expose
def index(self):
    # Retrieve the author stored in the current session
    # None if not defined
    author = cherrypy.session.get('author', None)

    page = [_header]

    if author:
        page.append("""
        <div><span>Hello %s, please leave us a note.
        <a href="author">Switch identity</a>.</span></div>"""
            %(author,))
        page.append(_note_form)
    else:
        page.append("""<div><a href="author">Set your
                    identity</a></span></div>""")

    notes = _notes[:]
    notes.reverse()
    for note in notes:
        page.append(self._render_note(note))

    page.append(_footer)
    # Returns to the CherryPy server the page to render
    return page

@cherrypy.expose
def note(self, id):
    # Retrieve the note attached to the given id
    try:
        note = _notes[int(id)]
    except:
        # If the ID was not valid, let's tell the
        # client we did not find it
        raise cherrypy.NotFound
    return [_header, self._render_note(note), _footer]

@cherrypy.expose
def post(self, text):
    author = cherrypy.session.get('author', None)

    # Here if the author was not in the session
    # we redirect the client to the author form
```

```
        if not author:
            raise cherrypy.HTTPRedirect('/author')
        note = Note(author, text)
        _notes.append(note)
        note.id = _notes.index(note)
        raise cherrypy.HTTPRedirect('/')

class Author(object):
    @cherrypy.expose
    def index(self):
        return [_header, _author_form, _footer]

    @cherrypy.expose
    def set(self, name):
        cherrypy.session['author'] = name
        return [_header, """
        Hi %s. You can now leave <a href="/" title="Home">notes</a>.
""" % (name,), _footer]


if __name__ == '__main__':
    # Define the global configuration settings of CherryPy
    global_conf = {
        'global': { 'engine.autoreload.on': False,
                    'server.socket_host': 'localhost',
                    'server.socket_port': 8080,
                  }}
    application_conf = {
        '/style.css': {
            'tools.staticfile.on': True,
            'tools.staticfile.filename': os.path.join(_curdir,
                                                      'style.css'),
            }
        }
    # Update the global CherryPy configuration
    cherrypy.config.update(global_conf)

    # Create an instance of the application
    note_app = NoteApp()
    # attach an instance of the Author class to the main application
    note_app.author = Author()

    # mount the application on the '/' base path
    cherrypy.tree.mount(note_app, '/', config = application_conf)
```

```
# Start the CherryPy HTTP server
cherrypy.server.quickstart()
# Start the CherryPy engine
cherrypy.engine.start()
```

Following is the CSS which should be saved in a file named `style.css` and stored in the same directory as `note.py`.

```
html, body {
    background-color: #DEDEDE;
    padding: 0px;
    marging: 0px;
    height: 100%;
}

.container {
    border-color: #A1A1A1;
    border-style: solid;
    border-width: 1px;
    background-color: #FFF;
    margin: 10px 150px 10px 150px;
    height: 100%;
}

a:link {
    text-decoration: none;
    color: #A1A1A1;
}

a:visited {
    text-decoration: none;
    color: #A1A1A1;
}

a:hover {
    text-decoration: underline;
}

input {
    border: 1px solid #A1A1A1;
}

.form {
    margin: 5px 5px 5px 5px;
}
```

```
.info {
    font-size: 70%;
    color: #A1A1A1;
}
```

In the rest of this chapter we will refer to the application to explain CherryPy's design.

Built-In HTTP Server

CherryPy comes with its own web (HTTP) server. The goal of this decision was to make CherryPy self-contained and allow users to run a CherryPy application within minutes of getting the library. As the name implies, the web server is the gateway to a CherryPy application through which all HTTP requests and responses have to go. It is therefore up to that layer to handle the low-level TCP sockets used to convey the information between the client and the server.

It is not compulsory to use the built-in server though and CherryPy is quite able to interface itself with other web servers if needed. Throughout this book, however, we will only use the default built-in web server.

To start the web server you have to make the following call:

```
cherrypy.server.quickstart()
```

Internal Engine

The CherryPy engine is the layer in charge of the following:

- Creating and managing Request and Response objects
  - ○ The Request is in charge of retrieving and calling the page handler matching the Request-URI.
  - ○ The Response object constructs and validates the response before handing it back to the underlying server.
- Controlling, managing, and monitoring the CherryPy process

To start the engine you must issue the following call:

```
cherrypy.engine.start()
```

Configuration

CherryPy comes with its own configuration system allowing you to parameterize the HTTP server as well as the behavior of the CherryPy engine when processing a Request-URI.

The settings can be stored either in a text file with syntax close to the INI format or in a pure Python dictionary. Choosing between the two is a matter of taste as both carry the same information.

CherryPy offers two entry points for passing configuration values—globally to the server instance through the cherrypy.config.update() method and per application via the cherrypy.tree.mount() method. In addition there is a third scope where configuration settings can be applied: per path.

To configure the CherryPy server instance itself you will need to use the global section of the settings.

In the note application we have defined the following settings:

```
global_conf = {
        'global': {

            'server.socket_host': 'localhost',
            'server.socket_port': 8080,

        },
}
application_conf = {
        '/style.css': {
            'tools.staticfile.on': True,
            'tools.staticfile.filename': os.path.join(_curdir,
                                                'style.css'),
        }
    }
```

This could be represented in a file like this:

```
[global]

server.socket_host="localhost"
server.socket_port=8080


[/style.css]
tools.staticfile.on=True
tools.staticfile.filename="/full/path/to.style.css"
```

When using a file to store the settings you must use valid Python objects (string, integer, Boolean, etc.).

We define the host and the port on which the server will listen for incoming connections.

Then we indicate to the CherryPy engine that the `/style.css` file is to be handled by the `staticfile` tool and also indicate the absolute path of the physical file to be served. We will explain in detail what tools are in the following chapters but for now imagine them as a way to extend CherryPy's internal features and enhance its possibilities.

To notify CherryPy of our global settings we need to make the following call:

- With a dictionary

  ```
  cherrypy.config.update(conf)
  ```

- With a file

  ```
  cherrypy.config.update('/path/to/the/config/file')
  ```

We also have to pass the configuration values to the mounted applications as follows:

- With a dictionary

  ```
  cherrypy.tree.mount(application_instance, script_name, config=conf)
  ```

- With a file

  ```
  cherrypy.tree.mount(application_instance, script_name,
                      config='/path/to/config/file')
  ```

Although in most cases choosing between a dictionary and a file will be a matter of taste, it may happen in some cases that one is better than the other. For instance, you may be required to pass complex data or objects to one key of the configuration, which cannot be achieved via a text file. On the other hand if the settings are to be amendable by the administrator of the application, using an INI file may facilitate that task.

 Remember that if you configure parts of your application such as we do to serve the stylesheet in our Note application, you must make a call to `cherrypy.tree.mount()`.

The last way of configuring your application is by using the _cp_config attribute on your page handler or as a class attribute of the class containing the page handlers, in which case the configuration will prevail for all page handlers.

In the following code sample, we indicate that all the page handlers of the Root class will use gzip compression except the hello page handler.

```
import cherrypy

class Root:
    _cp_config = {'tools.gzip.on': True}

    @cherrypy.expose
    def index(self):
        return "welcome"

    @cherrypy.expose
    def default(self, *args, **kwargs):
        return "oops"

    @cherrypy.expose
    # this next line is useless because we have set the class
    # attribute _cp_config but shows you how to configure a tool
    # using its decorator. We will explain more in the next
    # chapters.
    @cherrypy.tools.gzip()
    def echo(self, msg):
        return msg

    @cherrypy.expose
    def hello(self):
        return "there"
    hello._cp_config = {'tools.gzip.on': False}

if __name__ == '__main__':
    cherrypy.quickstart(Root(), '/')
```

The call to quickstart above is a shortcut for:

```
cherrypy.tree.mount(Root(), '/')
cherrypy.server.quickstart()
cherrypy.engine.start()
```

You can use this call anytime you only mount one single application on a CherryPy server.

The last important point is that configuration settings are independent of the prefix on which the application is mounted. Therefore in the above example even though the application could be mounted at /myapp instead of /, the settings would not be different. They would not include the prefix. Therefore consider the configuration settings to be relative to the application but independent of the prefix used to mount the application.

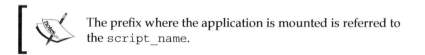

> The prefix where the application is mounted is referred to the script_name.

Object Publisher Engine

HTTP servers such as Apache or lighttpd map Request-URIs to paths on the file system making them very efficient at handling websites mainly made of static content such as images.

CherryPy has chosen a completely different approach and uses its own internal lookup algorithm to retrieve the handler referred to by the Request-URI. The decision made with CherryPy 2.0 was that such a handler would be a Python-callable object attached to a tree of published objects. That is the reason why we speak of object publishing as the Request-URI maps to a Python object.

CherryPy defines two important concepts:

- **Published**: A Python object is said to be published when it is attached to a tree of objects and the root of this tree is mounted on the CherryPy engine server via a call to cherrypy.tree.mount.

  For instance:
  ```
  root = Blog()
  root.admin = Admin()
  cherrypy.tree.mount(root, '/blog')
  ```

In the above example the root object is said to be published. By extension the admin object, which is an attribute of a published object, is also published.

- **Exposed**: A published object is said to be exposed when it has an attribute named exposed set to True. An exposed object must be Python callable.

  Being published is not sufficient for an object to be treated as being a potential handler for a URI by CherryPy. A published object must be exposed so that it becomes visible to the CherryPy engine. For instance:

```
class Root:
    @cherrypy.expose
    def index(self):
        return self.dosome()

    def dosome(self):
        return "hello there"
cherrypy.tree.mount(Root(), '/')
```

In this example a request to /dosome would return a **Not Found** error because the method is not exposed even though it belongs to a published object. The reason is that the dosome callable object is not exposed to the internal engine as a potential match for a URI.

You can set the exposed attribute either manually or by using the expose decorator provided by CherryPy as we will do throughout this book.

 An exposed object is usually referred to as a **page handler** by the CherryPy community. This is the term we will be using throughout the book.

For example, in the Note application the published objects are note_app and author. The root of the tree is note_app and is mounted on the '/' prefix. Therefore CherryPy will use that tree of objects upon receiving a request for any path starting with '/'. Had we used a prefix such as /postit, the Note application would have only been served by CherryPy when getting a request starting with such a prefix.

It is therefore possible to mount several applications via distinct prefixes. CherryPy will call the correct one based on the Request-URI. (As we will explain later in the book, two applications mounted via cherrypy.tree.mount() are unaware of each other. CherryPy makes sure that they don't leak.)

The following table displays the relationship between a Request-URI and the page handler matching the path of the URI as found by CherryPy.

Request-URI Path	Published Object	Page Handler
/	note_app	index
/author/	note_app.author	index
/author/set	note_app.author	set
/note/1	note_app	note

The index() and default() methods are special page handlers for CherryPy. The former one matches Request-URIs ending with a slash, similarly to the index.html file on the Apache server. The latter one is used by CherryPy when no explicit page handler is found for a Request-URI. Our Note application does not define one but the default page handler is often used to catch irregular URIs.

You can also notice that the /note/1 URI, in fact, matches note(id); this is because CherryPy supports positional parameters. The bottom line is that CherryPy will call the first page handler that has a signature matching the requested URI.

CherryPy treats /note/1 and /note?id=1 the same way as long as it finds a page handler with the following signature: note(id).

The following figure is a global overview of the process followed by an HTTP request when reaching the CherryPy server.

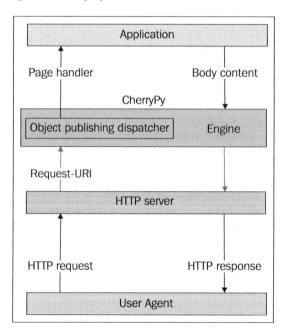

Library

CherryPy comes with a set of modules covering common tasks when building a web application such as session management, static resource service, encoding handling, or basic caching.

The Autoreload Feature

CherryPy is a long-running Python process, meaning that if we modify a Python module of the application, it will not be propagated in the existing process. Since stopping and restarting the server manually can be a tedious task, the CherryPy team has included an autoreload module that restarts the process as soon as it detects a modification to a Python module imported by the application. This feature is handled via configuration settings.

If you need the autoreload module to be enabled while in production you will set it up as below. Note the `engine.autoreload_frequency` option that sets the number of seconds the autoreloader engine has to wait before checking for new changes. It defaults to one second if not present.

```
[global]
server.environment = "production"
engine.autoreload_on = True
engine.autoreload_frequency = 5
```

Autoreload is not properly a module but we mention it here as it is a common feature offered by the library.

The Caching Module

Caching is an important side of any web application as it reduces the load and stress of the different servers in action—HTTP, application, and database servers. In spite of being highly correlated to the application itself, generic caching tools such as the ones provided by this module can help in achieving decent improvements in your application's performance.

The CherryPy caching module works at the HTTP server level in the sense that it will cache the generated output to be sent to the user agent and will retrieve a cached resource based on a predefined key, which defaults to the complete URL leading to that resource. The cache is held in the server memory and is therefore lost when stopping it. Note that you can also pass your own caching class to handle the underlying process differently while keeping the same high-level interface.

The Coverage Module

When building an application it is often beneficial to understand the path taken by the application based on the input it processes. This helps to determine potential bottlenecks and also see if the application runs as expected. The coverage module provided by CherryPy does this and provides a friendly browseable output showing the lines of code executed during the run. The module is one of the few that rely on a third-party package to run.

The Encoding/Decoding Module

Publishing over the Web means dealing with the multitude of existing character encoding. To one extreme you may only publish your own content using US-ASCII without asking for readers' feedback and to the other extreme you may release an application such as bulletin board that will handle any kind of charset. To help in this task CherryPy provides an encoding/decoding module that filters the input and output content based on server or user-agent settings.

The HTTP Module

This module offers a set of classes and functions to handle HTTP headers and entities.

For example, to parse the HTTP request line and query string:

```
s = 'GET /note/1 HTTP/1.1' # no query string
r = http.parse_request_line(s) # r is now ('GET', '/note/1', '',
                                           'HTTP/1.1')
s = 'GET /note?id=1 HTTP/1.1' # query string is id=1
r = http.parse_request_line(s) # r is now ('GET', '/note', 'id=1',
                                           'HTTP/1.1')
http.parseQueryString(r[2]) # returns {'id': '1'}
Provide a clean interface to HTTP headers:
For example, say you have the following Accept header value:
accept_value = "text/xml,application/xml,application/xhtml+xml,text/
html;q=0.9,text/plain;q=0.8,image/png,*/*;q=0.5"
values = http.header_elements('accept', accept_value)
print values[0].value, values[0].qvalue # will print text/html 1.0
```

The Httpauth Module

This module provides an implementation of the basic and digest authentication algorithm as defined in RFC 2617.

The Profiler Module

This module features an interface to conduct a performance check of the application.

The Sessions Module

The Web is built on top of a stateless protocol, HTTP, which means that requests are independent of each other. In spite of that, a user can navigate an e-commerce website with the impression that the application more or less follows the way he or she would call the store to pass an order. The session mechanism was therefore brought to the Web to allow servers to keep track of users' information.

CherryPy's session module offers a straightforward interface to the application developer to store, retrieve, amend, and delete chunks of data from a session object. CherryPy comes natively with three different back-end storages for session objects:

Back-end type	Advantages	Drawbacks
RAM	Efficient Accepts any type of objects No configuration needed	Information lost when server is shutdown Memory consumption can grow fast
File system	Persistence of the information Simple setup	File system locking can be inefficient Only serializable (via the pickle module) objects can be stored
Relational database (PostgreSQL built-in support)	Persistence of the information Robust Scalable Can be load balanced	Only serializable objects can be stored Setup less straightforward

The advantage is that your application will use a high-level interface independent of the underlying back end. Therefore, while in early development you may use RAM sessions, you can easily switch to the PostgreSQL back end if needed later on without modifying your application. Obviously CherryPy allows you to plug and use your own back end if needed.

The Static Module

Even the most dynamic application serves static resources such as images or CSS. CherryPy provides a module to ease the process of serving those or to even serve a complete directory structure. It will handle the underlying HTTP exchanges such as the use of the If-Modified-Since header, which checks if a resource has changed since a given date thus avoiding processing it again unnecessarily.

The Tidy Module

Even though as a web application developer you should make sure the content generated by your application is clean and valid against standards it may happen that you have to serve content over which you do not have full control. In such a case CherryPy provides an easy way to filter the outgoing content by using tools such as nsgml or tidy.

The Wsgiapp Module

This module allows you to wrap any WSGI application to use as a CherryPy application. For more information on WSGI, please refer to Chapter 4.

The XML-RPC Module

XML-RPC is a remote procedure call protocol using XML to format messages, transferred via HTTP, between an XML-RPC client and XML-RPC server. Basically, a client creates an XML document containing the name of the remote method to call and the values to be passed and then requests the server using an HTTP POST message. The returned HTTP response contains the XML document, as a string, to be processed by the client.

The CherryPy xmlrpc module allows you to transform a published object into an XML-RPC service. CherryPy will extract, from the incoming XML document, the name of the method as well as the values and will apply the same logic as if it was a regular URI call, therefore looking for a matching page handler. Then when the page handler returns CherryPy wraps the content into a valid XML-RPC response and sends it back to the client.

The following code sample defines an XML-RPC service served by CherryPy.

```
import cherrypy
from cherrypy import _cptools

class Root(_cptools.XMLRPCController):
    @cherrypy.expose
```

```
    def echo(self, message):
        return message

if __name__ == '__main__':
    cherrypy.quickstart(Root(), '/xmlrpc')
```

Your XML-RPC client could look like this:

```
import xmlrpclib
proxy = xmlrpclib.ServerProxy('http://localhost:8080/xmlrpc/')
proxy.echo('hello') # will return 'hello'
```

Tools

In the previous sections we have introduced the built-in modules. CherryPy provides a **unified interface**, referred as the **tool** interface, to call those modules or build and call your own modules.

Tools can be set up from three different contexts:

- The configuration file or dictionary

  ```
  conf = {'/': {
                  'tools.encode.on': True,
                  'tools.encode.encoding': 'ISO-8859-1'
              }
          }
  cherrypy.tree.mount(Root(), '/', config=conf)
  ```

- Attached to a particular page handler

  It is not uncommon to decide to add extra processing to an object path matching a URI. In that case you might want to use a Python decorator around the page handler.

  ```
  @cherrypy.expose
  @cherrypy.tools.encode(encoding='ISO 8859-1')
  def index(self)
          return "Et voilà"
  ```

- Making a library call with a higher-level interface

  Tools can be applied as regular Python callable objects.

  ```
  def index(self):
          cherrypy.tools.accept.callable(media='text/html')
  ```

The previous line shows how to call the accept tool that looks up the provided media type within the requested Accept HTTP header.

Thanks to that unified interface it is possible to modify the underlying code of the tool without having to modify the application level itself.

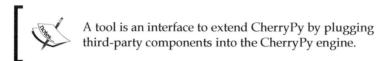

A tool is an interface to extend CherryPy by plugging third-party components into the CherryPy engine.

Error and Exception Handling

CherryPy tries hard to help the developer see a web application as close as a rich application. This means that from your page handler you may raise a Python error or exception as in any other Python application. CherryPy will catch those and transform them into HTTP messages depending on the type of errors.

Note that when an exception is raised and not caught by any other part of the application, CherryPy will return the corresponding HTTP 500 error code.

For example, the following example will show the default behavior of CherryPy.

```python
import cherrypy

class Root:
    @cherrypy.expose
    def index(self):
        raise NotImplementedError, "This is an error..."

if __name__ == '__main__':

    cherrypy.quickstart(Root(), '/')
```

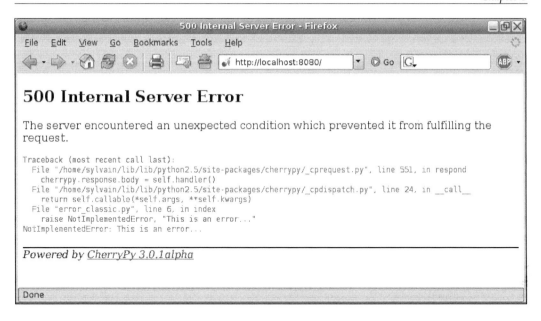

As you can see CherryPy displays the complete traceback of the Python error. Although this is useful when developing the application, it might not be relevant in production mode. In that case, CherryPy returns simply a default message.

 In development mode you can hide the tracebacks on error by using the `request.show_tracebacks` key in the `global` section of the configuration settings.

CherryPy returns an HTTP error code 500 when it catches an error that is not handled otherwise by the application developer. The HTTP specification defines two sets of error codes, client errors in the 4xx range and server errors in the 5xx range. The client errors indicate that the user agent has sent an invalid request (e.g. missing authentication credentials, requested resource not found or gone, etc.). The server errors inform the user agent that an event occurred that prevented the server fulfilling the request processing.

CherryPy provides a simple interface allowing the application developer to send the correct error code:

```
cherrypy.HTTPError(error_code, [error_message])
```

The HTTPError error will be trapped by the CherryPy engine, which will in turn use the error code and error message of the error as the status and body of the HTTP response to be sent.

When raising that error, CherryPy sets the HTTP response body to the provided message and the HTTP header matching the error code defined.

```
import cherrypy

class Root:
    @cherrypy.expose
    def index(self):
        raise cherrypy.HTTPError(401, 'You are not authorized to \
                                 access this resource')

if __name__ == '__main__':
    cherrypy.quickstart(Root(), '/')
```

The returned HTTP response will be:

```
HTTP/1.x 401 Unauthorized
Date: Wed, 14 Feb 2007 11:41:55 GMT
Content-Length: 744
Content-Type: text/html
Server: CherryPy/3.0.1alpha
```

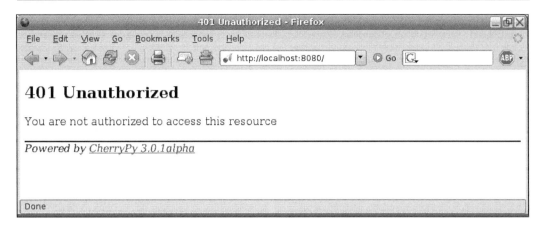

```
import cherrypy

class Root:
    @cherrypy.expose
    def index(self):
        # shortcut to cherrypy.HTTPError(404)
        raise cherrypy.NotFound

if __name__ == '__main__':
    conf = {'global':{'request.show_tracebacks':False}}
    cherrypy.config.update(conf)
    cherrypy.quickstart(Root(), '/')
```

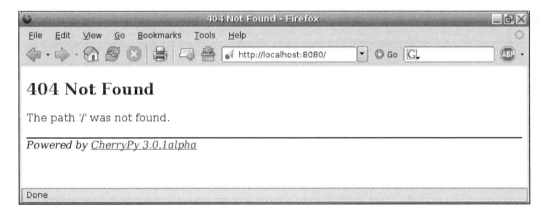

You might wonder how to change the layout of the error page returned by CherryPy to integrate it with your own application. The way to achieve this is by using the configuration system.

```python
import cherrypy

class Root:
    # Uncomment this line to use this template for this level of the
    # tree as well as its sub-levels
    #_cp_config = {'error_page.404': 'notfound.html'}
    @cherrypy.expose
    def index(self):
        raise cherrypy.NotFound

    # Uncomment this line to tell CherryPy to use that html page only
    # for this page handler. The other page handlers will use
    # the default CherryPy layout
    # index._cp_config = {'error_page.404': 'notfound.html'}


if __name__ == '__main__':
    # Globally set the new layout for an HTTP 404 error code
    cherrypy.config.update({'global':{'error_page.404':
                                      'notfound.html' }})
    cherrypy.quickstart(Root(), '/')
```

The `notfound.html` **page:**

```html
<html>
  <head><title>Clearly not around here</title></head>
  <body>
   <p>Well sorry but couldn't find the requested resource.</p>
  </body>
</html>
```

When catching an `HTTPError` error CherryPy looks for an `error_page.xxx` (where xxx is the HTTP error code used) entry in the configuration for that page handler and uses it instead of the default template.

As you can see CherryPy offers a very flexible and yet effective way to use your own page template for displaying friendlier error messages.

Until now we have discussed the high-level handling of errors in CherryPy. However, it is possible to modify the internal processing used through the hook API as we will see in the next chapter.

Summary

This chapter should have introduced you to some of the core principles of CherryPy, HTTP, and the server engine as well as its configuration system. We have also briefly discussed the object publisher engine, which allows transparent mapping of a URI to an exposed Python object. Finally we briefly reviewed the core modules of the CherryPy library that enhance its capacities and the way CherryPy lets you handle errors. The next chapter will dive into CherryPy's internal components and features as well go into more detail about some topics already covered.

4
CherryPy in Depth

Chapter 3 introduced the common aspects of CherryPy without going into too much detail. In this chapter, we will dive into what makes CherryPy such a powerful library for the web developer by explaining key features, such as how to run multiple HTTP servers, use additional URI dispatchers, use the built-in tools and develop new ones, serve static contents, and finally how CherryPy and WSGI interact. This chapter will be dense but will be a good base to allow you to be more at ease and efficient with the product.

HTTP Compliance

CherryPy has been evolving slowly but surely to comply as much as it can with the HTTP specifications—firstly by supporting the old HTTP/1.0 and then moving gradually towards fully supporting HTTP/1.1, as defined in RFC 2616. CherryPy is said to be conditionally compliant with HTTP/1.1 as it implements all the *must* and *required* levels but not all the *should* levels of the specification. Therefore, CherryPy supports the following features of HTTP/1.1:

- If a client claims to support HTTP/1.1, it must send a `Host` header field in any request made with that protocol version. If it is not done, CherryPy will immediately stop the request processing with a `400` error code message (section 14.23 of RFC 2616).

- CherryPy generates a `Date` header field in all the configurations (section 14.18 of RFC 2616).

- CherryPy does handle the `Continue` response status code (`100`) on clients supporting it.

- CherryPy's built-in HTTP server supports persistent connections that are the default in HTTP/1.1, through the use of the `Connection: Keep-Alive` header. Be aware that changing the HTTP server (for more details refer to Chapter 10) may break this compatibility, if the chosen server does not support such a feature.

- CherryPy handles correctly chunked requests and responses.
- CherryPy supports requests set with If-Modified-Since and If-Unmodified-Since headers and responds accordingly to each of them.
- CherryPy allows any HTTP methods.
- CherryPy handles all the combinations of HTTP versions between the client and the setting set for the server.

Request Protocol	Server Protocol	Written Response Protocol	Response Feature Set
1.0	1.0	1.0	1.0
1.0	1.1	1.1	1.0
1.1	1.0	1.0	1.0
1.1	1.1	1.1	1.1

The server protocol can be modified via the server.protocol_version key.

The written response protocol is the version returned in the HTTP response to inform the user-agent what protocol the server is supporting.

The response feature set protocol version is the one used internally by CherryPy during the response processing. In the second case, CherryPy only limits what it does to the response to HTTP/1.0.

All in all CherryPy 3 offers a wide range of capabilities, thanks to its good support of HTTP/1.1, and therefore can be safely used in a large set of scenarios.

Multiple HTTP Servers

By default, CherryPy starts a single instance of its own built-in HTTP server. However, it may happen that:

- You are required to have a different HTTP server. This will be covered extensively in Chapter 10.
- You are required to run your application on different network interfaces in one single Python process. CherryPy provides an API to run different HTTP server instances in one single process.

First let us see how the CherryPy server is usually started:

```
conf = {'global': {'server.socket_port': 100100,
                    'server.socket_host': 'localhost'}}
cherrypy.config.update(conf)
cherrypy.server.quickstart()
```

As you can see, we call the `quickstart()` method of the server object, which will instantiate the built-in HTTP server and start it in its own thread.

Now imagine we have one application that we wish to run on different network interfaces; we should do as follows:

```
from cherrypy import _cpwsgi

# Create a server on interface 1102.168.0.12 port 100100
s1 = _cpwsgi.CPWSGIServer()
s1.bind_addr = ('1102.168.0.12', 100100)

# Create a server on interface 1102.168.0.27 port 4700
s2 = _cpwsgi.CPWSGIServer()
s2.bind_addr = ('1102.168.0.27', 4700)

# Inform CherryPy which servers to start and use
cherrypy.server.httpservers = {s1: ('1102.168.0.12', 100100),
                               s2: ('1102.168.0.27', 4700)}
cherrypy.server.start()
```

As you can see, we first create two instances of the built-in HTTP server and for each we set the binding address on which the socket should be listening for incoming requests.

Then we attach those servers to the CherryPy pool of HTTP servers and call the `start()` method, which will start each one on its interface.

Notice that we do not call `cherrypy.config.update`, because it would update the global configuration settings shared by all the servers. However, this is not really an issue because each instance of the built-in server has the attributes matching the configuration keys. Thus:

```
s1.socket_port = 100100
s1.socket_host = '1102.168.0.12'
s1.socket_file = ''
s1.socket_queue_size = 5
s1.socket_timeout = 10
s1.protocol_version = 'HTTP/1.1'
s1.reverse_dns = False
s1.thread_pool = 10
s1.max_request_header_size = 500 * 1024
```

```
s1.max_request_body_size = 100 * 1024 * 1024
s1.ssl_certificate = None
s1.ssl_private_key = None
```

As you can see, you can directly set the server instance settings and avoid using the global configuration. This technique also allows for an application to be served via HTTP and HTTPS at the same time as we will see in Chapter 10.

Multi-Threaded Application Server

CherryPy is designed around the threaded pattern. Although it is transparent to the developer, each time the application gets or sets a value into the CherryPy namespace, (cherrypy.request and cherrypy.response objects mainly) it does so in a multi-threaded environment. Both cherrypy.request and cherrypy.response are thread-data containers, which imply that your application calls them independently by knowing which request is proxied through them at run time.

When using the built-in CherryPy server, a pool of threads is created to handle incoming requests. The size of the pool is configured via the server.thread_pool key, which defaults to 10. Although it could sound like a good idea to create a larger pool of threads to improve the performance of the server, it is not always the case.

This value must be tuned as per application requirements. In fact if your application has a very short average request processing time, then it is likely that each thread will not be busy for a very long period of time. If you create a large pool of threads, it is more likely that most of them will just sit there, consuming your memory for very little benefit. It is therefore advisable to run performance testing against your application in different configurations in order to determine the best number of threads that should be created for your requirements.

Application servers using the threaded pattern are not always highly regarded because the use of threads is seen as increasing the likelihood of problems due to synchronization requirements. Alternatives exist, such as:

- Multi-processes pattern: In this case, each request is handled by its own Python process. It is arguable that synchronization is easier but in some specific cases the performance and stability of the server can be better.
- Asynchronous pattern: In this configuration, the operation of accepting new connections and sending back data to the client is done asynchronously from the request processing itself. This can be achieved, thanks to the capabilities of underlying operating systems allowing it. This technique has proven to be very efficient speed-wise. However, it requires a fairly different application development approach that can perturb some developers.

All in all, which solution is the best can be debated ad infinitum and such questions will never really be answered. In fact, each scenario requires a different approach.

URI Dispatching

As we have seen in the Chapter 3, by default CherryPy maps URIs to Python callables that have an `exposed` attribute set to `True`. Over time, it has appeared that the CherryPy community wants to be more flexible and that other dispatchers' solutions would be appreciated. That's why CherryPy 3 provides three other built-in dispatchers and offers a simple way to write and use your own dispatchers.

- One is set to allow applications to be developed per HTTP methods. (GET, POST, PUT, etc.)

- The second is based on a popular third-party package named Routes and developed by Ben Bangert from the original Ruby implementation for Ruby on Rails.

- The third dispatcher is a Virtual Host one, which allows dispatching based on the domain requested rather than the URI path.

HTTP Method Dispatcher

In some applications, URIs are independent of the action to be performed by the server on the resource. For example, look at the following URI:

```
http://somehost.com/album/delete/12
```

As you can see, the URI contains the operation the client wishes to carry out. With the default CherryPy dispatcher this would map to something like:

```
album.delete(12)
```

Although it's fine, you may wish to remove that operation from the URI itself and make it more independent, so that it would look like:

```
http://somehost.com/album/12
```

You may wonder immediately how the server is supposed to know which operation to perform. This information is carried by the HTTP request itself, thanks to the HTTP method:

```
DELETE /album/12 HTTP/1.1
```

The page handler handling such a request would look like the following:

```
class Album:
    exposed = True

    def GET(self, id):
        ....

    def POST(self, title, description):
        ....

    def PUT(self, id, title, description):
        ....

    def DELETE(self, id):
        ....
```

When using the HTTP method dispatcher, the page handler called would be `album.DELETE(12)`.

If you look at the previous class definition, you will see that the methods do not carry the `exposed` attribute but instead the class itself is set with that attribute. The reason for this comes from the way the dispatcher is implemented.

When a request reaches the server, CherryPy looks for the best matching page handler. When using the HTTP method dispatcher, the handler is in fact the conceptual representation of the resource targeted by the URI, in our example the instance of the `album` class. Then the dispatcher checks if the class has a method matching the name of the HTTP method used for the request. If so, the dispatcher calls it with the remaining parameters. Otherwise, it sends back immediately an HTTP error code `405 Method Not Allowed` to inform the client that it cannot use the HTTP method and thus cannot perform that operation on that particular resource.

For example, if we did not have a definition for `DELETE` in the `Album` class, such an error code would be returned upon the request we have used so far.

In any case, however, CherryPy will automatically add the `Allow` HTTP header to the response to inform the client which methods it can use against the resource.

Note that in this case CherryPy does not look for `index` or `default` page handlers as it would with the URI-to-object dispatcher. This comes from a fundamental difference between dispatching based on the URI solely as compared to the URI+HTPP method. Chapter 6 will review this in more detail.

To enable the HTTP method dispatcher, you must set the `request.dispatch` key to an instance of that dispatcher for the targeted path.

For example, if our whole application was built using that technique, we would use:

```
{'/' : {'request.dispatch':  cherrypy.dispatch.MethodDispatcher()}}
```

The HTTP method dispatcher is often used in applications following REST principles, as we will see in Chapter 6.

Routes Dispatcher

Whether in the URI-to-object or HTTP-method dispatcher, we have not explicitly declared the URI associated with a page handler; instead we have left the responsibility of finding the best correspondence to the CherryPy engine. Many developers prefer the explicit approach and decide how URIs should map to page handlers.

Therefore, when using the Routes dispatcher you must connect a pattern that matches URIs and associates a specific page handler.

Let's review an example:

```python
import cherrypy

class Root:
    def index(self):
        return "Not much to say"

    def hello(self, name):
        return "Hello %s" % name

if __name__ == '__main__':
    root = Root()

    # Create an instance of the dispatcher
    d = cherrypy.dispatch.RoutesDispatcher()

    # connect a route that will be handled by the 'index' handler
    d.connect('default_route', '', controller=root)

    # connect a route to the 'hello' handler
    # this will match URIs such as '/say/hello/there'
    # but not '/hello/there'
    d.connect('some_other', 'say/:action/:name',
                controller=root, action='hello')

    # set the dispatcher
    conf = {'/': {'request.dispatch': d}}
    cherrypy.quickstart(root, '/', config=conf)
```

When using the Routes dispatcher handlers, you need not have an exposed attribute.

The `connect` method of the Routes dispatcher is defined as:

```
connect(name, route, controller, **kwargs)
```

Here are the parameters for the `connect` method:

- The `name` parameter is the unique name for the route to connect.
- The `route` is the pattern to match URIs.
- The `controller` is the instance containing page handlers.
- `**kwargs` allows you to pass on extra valid parameters for a route.

Please refer to the official Routes documentation to understand how the package works.

By default, the CherryPy Routes dispatcher does not pass on the `action` and `controller` values returned by the Routes mapper when matching a URI against any of the route. These are not necessarily useful in a CherryPy application. However, if you need them you can set the `fetch_result` parameter of the Routes dispatcher constructor to `True`. Then both values will be passed on to page handlers but in this case you will have to add `controller` and `action` parameters to all your page handlers.

Virtual Host Dispatcher

It may happen that you need to host different web applications within one CherryPy server with each application serving one given domain name. CherryPy provides an easy way to do this, as in the following example:

```
import cherrypy

class Site:
    def index(self):
        return "Hello, world"
    index.exposed = True


class Forum:
    def __init__(self, name):
        self.name = name
```

```
    def index(self):
        return "Welcome on the %s forum" % self.name
    index.exposed = True

if __name__ == '__main__':
    site = Site()
    site.cars = Forum('Cars')
    site.music = Forum('My Music')

    hostmap = {'www.ilovecars.com': '/cars',
               'www.mymusic.com': '/music',}

    cherrypy.config.update({'server.socket_port': 80})
    conf = {'/': {'request.dispatch':
                        cherrypy.dispatch.VirtualHost(**hostmap)}}
    cherrypy.tree.mount(site, config=conf)
    cherrypy.server.quickstart()
    cherrypy.engine.start()
```

First, as you can see, we simply create a tree of applications. Next, we define the `hostmap` dictionary, which will inform the `VirtualHost` dispatcher how to serve a request based on its domain. Thus the requests coming from www.mymusic.com will be served by the application mounted at the `/music` prefix. Next, we tell CherryPy that we will be using the `VirtualHost` dispatcher and we finally mount the site application and start the server as usual.

Note that this example will require that you edit your `hosts` file on your machine to add the following two domains:

```
127.0.0.1 www.ilovecars.com
127.0.0.1 www.mymusic.com
```

It will automatically redirect requests to those domains to your local server instead of looking for them on the Internet. Once you have finished with this example, you ought to remove these lines from the `hosts` file.

Hook into CherryPy's Core Engine

One of the most powerful aspects of CherryPy is how its core lets you modify its normal behavior with a very fine granularity. Indeed, CherryPy offers a mechanism called hooking to customize the core engine.

A **hook** is an entry point for Python callables to be applied at specific points during the request processing. CherryPy provides the following entry points:

Hook Point	Description
on_start_resource	Called at the beginning of the process.
before_request_body	Called before CherryPy tries to read the request body. It allows a tool to inform CherryPy whether this action should be performed by setting the process_request_body attribute to False within the tool.
before_handler	Called before the page handler is invoked. A tool could for instance set the handler to None to inform CherryPy that it should not process the page handler.
before_finalize	Called whether or not the page handler has been called and before CherryPy starts processing the response.
on_end_resource	Called when the resource processing is terminated.
before_error_response after_error_response	Called when an error is trapped by the CherryPy engine to allow the application to recover and decide what to do next.
on_end_request	Called at the end of the overall processing, right after the link with the client has been closed. This allows you to free resources.

The following figure shows the global process followed by CherryPy when handling a request. The black lines and arrows show the normal flow while the gray ones indicate the path when an error occurs.

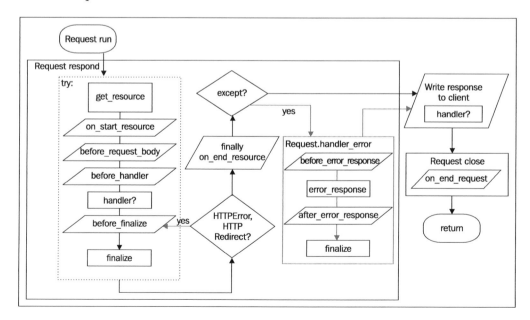

Attaching a callback at one of these hook points is done via a call to:

```
cherrypy.request.hooks.attach(point, callback, failsafe=None,
                              priority=None, **kwargs)
```

The first parameter is the name of the hook point as shown in the previous table. The second parameter is the Python callable that will be applied. The third parameter indicates to CherryPy that even if another callback may fail during the processing of this hook point, CherryPy must run this callable. The last parameter must be a value between 0 and 100 to indicate the weight of each callback and provide a way to order them. Lower values will be run first.

The failsafe argument is quite helpful as it offers a way for an application to be flexible and recover from problems that may occur. Indeed some callbacks may fail without impacting the whole chain of the request processing.

 Note that you can obviously attach as many callbacks as required at a given hook point. Callbacks can be hooked on the fly while the application is running as well. However, the more callbacks you attach, the slower the processing of that hook point will become.

The hooking mechanism is fairly close to what used to be called filters in CherryPy 2. However, it was observed over time that they were too low level and were making users uncomfortable most of the time. That's why it is still rare for developers to use them directly as is. Instead they are applied through a higher-level interface named tools.

CherryPy Toolbox

The tool interface has been designed by Robert Brewer while refactoring CherryPy. The goal was to offer ready-to-employ tools achieving common tasks with a friendly and flexible API. Within CherryPy, built-in tools offer a single interface to call the CherryPy library that we have reviewed in Chapter 3 using the hooking mechanism.

As we have seen in Chapter 3 tools can be used in three different ways:

- From the configuration settings
- As a Python decorator or via the special _cp_config attribute of a page handler
- As a Python callable that can be applied from within any function

Thanks to this flexibility, a tool can be set either globally to a path and its subset or to a particular page handler. Let's now review the built-in tools provided by CherryPy.

Basic Authentication Tool

Purpose: The purpose of this tool is to provide basic authentication (RFC 2617) to your application.

Arguments:

Name	Default	Description
realm	N/A (N/A in this case means the parameter must be provided by the developer as it has no default.)	String defining the realm value.
users	N/A	Dictionary of the form–username:password or a Python callable returning such a dictionary.
encrypt	None	Python callable used to encrypt the password returned by the client and compare it with the encrypted password provided in the users dictionary. If None it uses an MD5 hash.

Example:

```
import sha
import cherrypy

class Root:
    @cherrypy.expose
    def index(self):
        return """<html>
<head></head>
<body>
  <a href="admin">Admin area</a>
</body>
</html>
"""

class Admin:
    @cherrypy.expose
    def index(self):
        return "This is a private area"

if __name__ == '__main__':
```

```
def get_users():
    # 'test': 'test'
    return {'test':
                'a104a8fe5ccb110ba61c4c0873d3101e10871082fbbd3'}

def encrypt_pwd(token):
    return sha.new(token).hexdigest()

conf = {'/admin': {'tools.basic_auth.on': True,
                   'tools.basic_auth.realm': 'Some site',
                   'tools.basic_auth.users': get_users,
                   'tools.basic_auth.encrypt': encrypt_pwd}}
root = Root()
root.admin = Admin()
cherrypy.quickstart(root, '/', config=conf)
```

The get_users function returns a hard-coded dictionary but it could also fetch the values from a database or anywhere else. Keep in mind that the basic authentication scheme is not really secure as the password is only encoded and can be decoded on the fly if someone captures it. This scheme is, however, often used over SSL because it is the easiest to put in place while the Secure Socket Layer encrypts the enclosed data.

Caching Tool

Purpose: The purpose of this tool is to provide basic in-memory caching of CherryPy generated content.

Arguments:

Name	Default	Description
invalid_methods	("POST", "PUT", "DELETE")	Tuples of strings of HTTP methods not to be cached. These methods will also invalidate (delete) any cached copy of the resource.
cache_class	MemoryCache	Class object to be used for caching.

A comprehensive example would be out of the scope of this book but if you are interested in this tool you should first look at the CherryPy test suite as well as visit the CherryPy users' mailing-list.

Decoding Tool

Purpose: The purpose of this tool is to decode the incoming request parameters.

Arguments:

Name	Default	Description
encoding	None	What encoding is to be used to decode the incoming content? If None it looks for the Content-Type header and if it cannot find a suitable charset it uses default_encoding.
default_encoding	"UTF-8"	Default encoding to be used when none is provided or found.

Example:

```
import cherrypy
from cherrypy import tools

class Root:
    @cherrypy.expose
    def index(self):
        return """<html>
<head></head>
<body>
  <form action="hello" method="post">
    <input type="text" name="name" value="" />
  </form>
</body>
</html>
"""

    @cherrypy.expose
    @tools.decode(encoding='ISO-88510-1')
    def hello(self, name):
        return "Hello %s" % (name, )

if __name__ == '__main__':
    cherrypy.quickstart(Root(), '/')
```

In this case when the HTML form is sent to the server, CherryPy tries to decode the incoming data using the encoding we have set. If you look at the type of the name parameter you will see that when using the decoding tool it is *Unicode* whereas without the tool it is a *string*.

Digest Authentication Tool

Purpose: The purpose of this tool is to provide digest authentication as defined in RFC 2617.

Arguments:

Name	Default	Description
realm	N/A	String defining the realm value.
users	N/A	Dictionary of the form—username:password or a Python callable returning such a dictionary.

Example:

```
import cherrypy

class Root:
    @cherrypy.expose
    def index(self):
        return """<html>
<head></head>
<body>
  <a href="admin">Admin area</a>
</body>
</html>
"""

class Admin:
    @cherrypy.expose
    def index(self):
        return "This is a private area"

if __name__ == '__main__':

    def get_users():
        return {'test': 'test'}

    conf = {'/admin': {'tools.digest_auth.on': True,
                       'tools.digest_auth.realm': 'Some site',
                       'tools.digest_auth.users': get_users}}
    root = Root()
    root.admin = Admin()
    cherrypy.quickstart(root, '/', config=conf)
```

Note that the digest tool does not provide a way to pass an encrypted password. The reason for this is that the digest scheme is defined not to send the password across the wire as clear text. The way it works is as follows:

1. The client requests to access the resource. The server returns a 401 error code indicating it uses the digest scheme. The server provides a token for this exchange.

2. The client creates a new message based on the token, the username, and the password and generates a hash via the MD5 algorithm.

3. Upon receiving the new message from the client, the server tries to generate the same values. If they all match, the authentication is allowed.

As you can see, the password never transits as clear text on the wire. Discussions have taken place to decide how the digest tool can be evolved in order to avoid the need to store passwords as clear text. One way would be to store one of the intermediate steps of the digest token (step 1) and compare this value with what has been sent by the client. This is beyond the scope of this book but you can get more information from the CherryPy mailing lists.

Encode Tool

Purpose: The purpose of this tool is to encode the response content in a defined encoding.

Arguments:

Name	Default	Description
encoding	None	What encoding is to be used to encode the response? If None, it looks for the Content-Type header and sets a suitable charset if it can.
errors	"strict"	Defines how the tool must react when it fails to encode a character.

Example:

```
import cherrypy
from cherrypy import tools

class Root:
    @cherrypy.expose
    def index(self):
        return """<html>
<head></head>
<body>
```

```
    <form action="hello" method="post">
      <input type="text" name="name" value="" />
    </form>
  </body>
  </html>
  """

      @cherrypy.expose
      @tools.encode(encoding='ISO-88510-15')
      def hello(self, name):
          return "Hello %s" % name

  if __name__ == '__main__':
      cherrypy.quickstart(Root(), '/')
```

Error Redirect Tool

Purpose: The purpose of this tool is to modify the default CherryPy error handler.

Arguments:

Name	Default	Description
url	"	The URL to which it should be redirected.
internal	True	When `True`, the redirection is hidden from the client and happens only within the context of this request. If `False`, CherryPy informs the client that a redirection should be issued by the client itself to the URL provided.

Etag Tool

Purpose: The purpose of this tool is to validate an **Entity Tag (Etag)** sent by a user agent and generate the response accordingly as defined by RFC 2616 section 14.24. Etags are one of the ways to cache HTTP responses and thus diminish the burden on any parties involved.

Argument:

Name	Default	Description
autotags	False	When `True` the tool will generate an `etag` value based on the response body set.

Example:

```
import cherrypy
from cherrypy import tools

class Root:
    @cherrypy.expose
    def index(self):
        return """<html>
<head></head>
<body>
  <form action="hello" method="post">
    <input type="text" name="name" value="" />
  </form>
</body>
</html>
"""

    @cherrypy.expose
    def hello(self, name):
        return "Hello %s" % name

if __name__ == '__main__':
    conf = {'/': {'tools.etags.on': True,
                  'tools.etags.autotags': True}}
    cherrypy.quickstart(Root(), '/', config=conf)
```

In the previous example, we set the etags tool for the whole application. On the first request to the index page handler, the tool will generate an etag value and insert it in the response headers. On the next request to that URI, the client will include the last received etag. The tool will compare it with the current one and if they match the response will be 304 Not Modified informing the client that it can safely use its copy of the resource.

Note that if you need the etag value to be computed in a different fashion, the best way is to set the autotags parameter to False, the default, and then from within your page handler add the Etag header yourself to the response headers.

Gzip Tool

Purpose: The purpose of this tool is to perform content encoding on the response body.

Arguments:

Name	Default	Description
compress_level	10	Level of compression to be achieved. The lower it is, the faster it will be.
mime_types	['text/html', 'text/plain']	List of MIME types that can be compressed.

Example:

```
import cherrypy
from cherrypy import tools

class Root:
    @cherrypy.expose
    @tools.gzip()
    def index(self):
        return "this will be compressed"

if __name__ == '__main__':
    cherrypy.quickstart(Root(), '/')
```

Note that the gzip tool should not be used when the response is streamed via its stream attribute. Indeed in this case CherryPy starts sending the body as soon as it has something to send, for instance when the page handler yields the content, instead of returning it.

Ignore Headers Tool

Purpose: The purpose of this tool is to remove the specified headers from the HTTP request before they are processed by CherryPy.

Argument:

Name	Default	Description
ignore_headers	headers=('Range',)	Tuple of header names to be disregarded.

Example:

```
import cherrypy
from cherrypy import tools

class Root:
    @cherrypy.expose
    @tools.ignore_headers(headers=('Accept-Language',))
    def index(self):
        return "Accept-Language: %s" \
                % cherrypy.request.headers.get('Accept-Language',
                                                'none provided')

    @cherrypy.expose
    def other(self):
        return "Accept-Language: %s" % cherrypy.request.headers.
get('Accept-Language')

if __name__ == '__main__':
    cherrypy.quickstart(Root(), '/')
```

If you access http://localhost:8080/, you will get the following message whether or not the client has indeed set that header:

```
Accept-Language: none provided
```

If you navigate to http://localhost:8080/other you will get the following message:

```
Accept-Language: en-us,en;q=0.5
```

Log Headers Tool

Purpose: The purpose of this tool is to dump request headers into the error log file when an error occurs on the server. This tool is disabled by default.

Argument: None

Example:

```
import cherrypy
from cherrypy import tools

class Root:
    @cherrypy.expose
    def index(self):
        raise StandardError, "Some sensible error message here"
```

```
if __name__ == '__main__':
    cherrypy.config.update({'global': {'tools.log_headers.on':
                                       True}})
    cherrypy.quickstart(Root(), '/')
```

When you access `http://localhost:8080`, the error will be raised and the error log will show the request headers. Note that in this case this tool is set at the web-server level via the `cherrypy.config.update()` method but it can be applied on a per path basis as well.

Log Tracebacks Tool

Purpose: The purpose of this tool is to dump the error's traceback into the error log file when an exception is raised. This tool is enabled by default.

Argument: None

Example:

```
import cherrypy
from cherrypy import tools

class Root:
    @cherrypy.expose
    def index(self):
        raise StandardError, "Some sensible error message here"


if __name__ == '__main__':
    # This tool is applied globally to the CherryPy process
    # by using the global cherrypy.config.update method.
    cherrypy.config.update({'global': {'tools.log_tracebacks.on':
                                       False}})
    cherrypy.quickstart(Root(), '/')
```

Proxy Tool

Purpose: The purpose of this tool is to change the base URL of the requests. This is especially helpful when running the application behind another server such as Apache.

Arguments:

Name	Default	Description
base	None	If set and `local` is none, this will be the new base URL available from `cherrypy.request.base`.
local	'X-Forwarded-Host'	Which header to look at for the local hosts set for instance by the front-end web server.
remote	'X-Forwarded-For'	Header to look for the IP address of the originating client.
scheme	'X-Forwarded-Proto'	Header to look for the original scheme used: *http* or *https* for instance.

When the base is not set, the tool will build the new base URI from the values fetched from the request headers based on the other parameters.

Example:

```
import cherrypy
from cherrypy import tools

class Root:
    @cherrypy.expose
    def index(self):
        return "Base URL: %s %s " % (cherrypy.request.base,
                                     cherrypy.url(''))


    @cherrypy.expose
    def other(self):
        raise cherrypy.HTTPRedirect(cherrypy.url(''))

if __name__ == '__main__':
    conf = {'global': {'tools.proxy.on': True,
                       'tools.proxy.base': 'http://someapp.net/blog',
                       'tools.proxy.local': ''}}
    cherrypy.config.update(conf)
    cherrypy.quickstart(Root(), '/')
```

When navigating to `http://localhost:8080` you will see the following message:

```
Base URL: http://someapp.net/blog http://someapp.net/blog/
```

If you navigate to `http://localhost:8080/other`, you will be redirected to `http://someapp.net/blog/`, which shows that the proxy tools ensure in a transparent manner that the CherryPy library stays coherent in behavior in accordance with the settings you provide.

For more examples on using this tool behind another server please see Chapter 10.

Referer Tool

Purpose: The purpose of this tool is to allow the filtering of requests based on a pattern. Requests can be rejected or accepted after matching the pattern.

Arguments:

Name	Default	Description
pattern	N/A	Regular expression pattern.
accept	True	If True any matching referer will allow the request to proceed. Otherwise, any matching referer will cause the request to be rejected.
accept_ missing	False	Whether requests with no referer can be allowed or not.
error	403	HTTP error code to be returned to the user agent upon refusal.
message	'Forbidden Referer header.'	Message to be returned to the user agent upon refusal.

Example:

```
import cherrypy
from cherrypy import tools

class Root:
    @cherrypy.expose
    def index(self):
        return cherrypy.request.headers.get('Referer')

if __name__ == '__main__':
    conf = {'/': {'tools.referer.on': True,
                  'tools.referer.pattern': 'http://[^/]*dodgy\.com',
                  'tools.referer.accept': False}}
    cherrypy.quickstart(Root(), '/', config=conf)
```

In this example, we will reject all requests coming from the `dodgy.com` domain and sub-domains.

Response Headers Tool

Purpose: The purpose of this tool is to allow some common headers to be set for all or many page handlers at once.

Argument:

Name	Default	Description
headers	None	List of tuples: header, value

Example:

```python
import cherrypy
from cherrypy import tools

class Root:
    @cherrypy.expose
    def index(self):
        return "Some text"

    @cherrypy.expose
    def other(self):
        return "Some other text"

if __name__ == '__main__':
    conf = {'/': {'tools.response_headers.on': True,
                  'tools.response_headers.headers': [('Content-Type',
                                                      'text/plain')]}}
    cherrypy.quickstart(Root(), '/', config=conf)
```

In this example, the tool sets Content-Type to text/plain for all page handlers.

Trailing Slash Tool

Purpose: The purpose of this tool is to provide a flexible way to deal with the trailing slash of requests. This tool is enabled by default.

Arguments:

Name	Default	Description
missing	True	If the page handler is the index, if the `missing` parameter is `True`, and if the request missed a trailing slash, CherryPy will automatically issue a redirection towards the URI with the additional slash at the end.
extra	False	If the page handler is not the index, if the `extra` parameter is set to `True`, and if the URI has a trailing slash, CherryPy will issue a redirection towards the URI without the trailing slash.

Example:

```
import cherrypy
from cherrypy import tools

class Root:
    @cherrypy.expose
    def index(self):
        return "This should have been redirected to add the trailing
                slash"

    @cherrypy.expose
    def nothing(self):
        return "This should have NOT been redirected"
    nothing._cp_config = {'tools.trailing_slash.on': False}

    @cherrypy.expose
    def extra(self):
        return "This should have been redirected to remove the
                trailing slash"
    extra._cp_config = {'tools.trailing_slash.on': True,
                        'tools.trailing_slash.missing': False,
                        'tools.trailing_slash.extra': True}

if __name__ == '__main__':
    cherrypy.quickstart(Root(), '/')
```

To understand this tool, navigate to the following URLs:

```
http://localhost:8080
```

```
http://localhost:8080/nothing
```

```
http://localhost:8080/nothing/
```

```
http://localhost:8080/extra/
```

XML-RPC Tool

Purpose: The purpose of this tool is to transform CherryPy into an XML-RPC server and make page handlers XML-RPC callables.

Argument: None

Example:

```
import cherrypy
from cherrypy import _cptools

class Root:
    @cherrypy.expose
    def index(self):
        return "Regular web page handler"

class XMLRPCApp(_cptools.XMLRPCController):
    @cherrypy.expose
    def echo(self, message):
        return message

if __name__ == '__main__':
    root = Root()
    root.xmlrpc = XMLRPCApp()
    cherrypy.quickstart(root, '/')
```

The XMLRPCController is a helper class that should be used instead of the XML-RPC tool directly.

You can then test your XML-RPC handler as follows:

```
>>> import xmlrpclib
>>> s = xmlrpclib.ServerProxy('http://localhost:8080/xmlrpc')
>>> s.echo('test')
'test'
```

Toolbox

CherryPy tools must belong to a toolbox that is to be managed by the CherryPy engine. Toolboxes have their own namespace to avoid name collision. Although nothing prevents you from using the default toolbox you can create one of your own as follows:

```
from cherrypy._cptools import Toolbox,
mytb = Toolbox('mytb')
mytb.xml_parse = Tool('before_handler', xmlparse)
conf = {'/': {'mytb.xml_parse.on': True,
              'mytb.xml_parse.engine': 'amara'}}
```

Creating a Tool

Now that we have reviewed the toolbox shipped with CherryPy, we will explain how to write a tool. Before deciding to create a tool you should ask yourself a few questions such as:

- Should the added feature be handled at the CherryPy level?
- At which level of the request processing should this be applied?
- Will you modify CherryPy's default behavior?

These questions simply allow you to make sure that the feature you want to add is at the right level. Tools can sometimes look like a pattern on their own, upon which you can design your application.

We will create a tool that will read and parse XML contained in a request body into a page handler parameter. To do so, we will be using the ElementTree library. (ElementTree is maintained by Fredrik Lundh and Amara by Uche Ogbuji.)

A tool is created either by sub-classing the `Tool` class or via an instance of that class as shown in the following example. Instantiating the `Tool` class is the most common case to consider and it is the one we will be discussing.

The class constructor declaration is as follows:

```
Tool(point, callable, name=None, priority=50)
```

- The `point` parameter is a string indicating to which hook point this tool should be attached.
- The `callable` parameter is a Python callable that will be applied.

- The `name` parameter defines what the name of the tool will be within the toolbox. When it is not provided, it uses the name of the attribute holding the instance of the tool within the toolbox (refer to our example).
- The `priority` sets the order of the tools when several tools are attached at the same hook point.

Once an instance of the tool is created, you can attach it to the built-in toolbox as follows:

```
cherrypy.tools.mytool = Tool('on_start_resource', mycallable)
```

This tool will be available like any other built-in tools to your application.

When creating a tool, you can provide two attributes to your callable that will be used when initializing the tool. They are as follows:

- `failsafe`: If `True`, it means the tool will run even when an error is raised before the tool's turn. It defaults to `False`.
- `priority`: Relative order of this tool in regards to others at the same hook point. It defaults to `50`.

Thus you could write:

```
def mycallable(...):
    ....
mycallable.failsafe = True
mycallable.priority = 30
cherrypy.tools.mytool = Tool('on_start_resource', mycallable)
```

CherryPy provides a shortcut for tools that will be applied at the `before_handler` hook point, in other words just before the page handler is called. This should be one of the most common cases for non-built-in tools.

```
cherrypy.tools.mytool = Tool('before_handler', mycallable)
```

This is equivalent to the following:

```
cherrypy.tools.mytool = HandlerTool(mycallable)
```

The `HandlerTool` class provides one additional feature as it allows your callable to be applied as a page handler itself through the `handler(*args, **kwargs)` method of the `HandlerTool` class. Thus:

```
class Root:
    other = cherrypy.tools.mytool.handler()
```

This can be useful to provide the same handler in different areas of your application without duplicating code.

Let's now see a more elaborate example:

```
import cherrypy
from cherrypy import tools
from cherrypy import Tool
from xml.parsers.expat import ExpatError
from xml.sax._exceptions import SAXParseException

def xmlparse(engine='elementtree', valid_content_types=['text/xml',
              'application/xml'], param_name='doc'):
    # Transform the XML document contained in the request body into
    # an instance of the chosen XML engine.

    # Get the mime type of the entity sent by the user-agent
    ct = cherrypy.request.headers.get('Content-Type', None)

    # if it is not a mime type we can handle
    # then let's inform the user-agent
    if ct not in valid_content_types:
        raise  cherrypy.HTTPError(415, 'Unsupported Media Type')

    # CherryPy will set the request.body with a file object
    # where to read the content from
    if hasattr(cherrypy.request.body, 'read'):
        content = cherrypy.request.body.read()
        doc = content
        try:
            if engine == 'elementtree':
                from elementtree import ElementTree as ETX
                doc = ETX.fromstring(content)
            elif engine == 'amara':
                import amara
                doc = amara.parse(content)
        except (ExpatError, SAXParseException):
            raise cherrypy.HTTPError(400, 'XML document not
                                    well-formed')

        # inject the parsed document instance into
        # the request parameters as if it had been
        # a regular URL encoded value
        cherrypy.request.params[param_name] = doc

    # Create a new Tool and attach it to the default CherryPy toolbox
```

```
tools.xml_parse = Tool('before_handler', xmlparse)

class Root:
    @cherrypy.expose
    @tools.xml_parse()
    def echoet(self, doc):
        return doc.find('.//message').text

    @cherrypy.expose
    @tools.xml_parse(engine='amara', param_name='d')
    def echoamara(self, d):
        return unicode(d.root.message)

if __name__ == '__main__':
    cherrypy.quickstart(Root(), '/')
```

 In order to test the tool, you will need ElementTree or Amara or both. You can install both via the `easy_install` command.

Our XML tool will read the HTTP body content and parse it via the specified XML toolkit. Then it will inject back the parsed document into the request parameters so that the new document instance is passed on to the page handler as a regular parameter.

Launch the previous example and then run in a Python interpreter:

```
>>> s = '<root><message>Hello!<message></root>'
>>> headers = {'Content-Type': 'application/xml'}

>>> import httplib
>>> conn = httplib.HTTPConnection("localhost:8080")

>>> conn.request("POST", "/echoet", s, headers)
>>> r1 = conn.getresponse()
>>> print r1.status, r1.reason
200 OK
>>> r1.read()
'Hello!'

>>> conn.request("POST", "/echoamara", s, headers)
>>> r1 = conn.getresponse()
>>> print r1.status, r1.reason
200 OK
>>> r1.read()
```

```
'Hello!'

>>> conn.request("POST", "/echoamara", s)
>>> r1 = conn.getresponse()
>>> print r1.status, r1.reason
415 Unsupported Media Type

>>> conn.close()
```

As you can see the tool interface provided by CherryPy 3 is powerful, flexible, and yet quite intuitive and easy to reuse. However, always be careful to ponder over your requirements before using tools. They should be used for low-level operations that fit into the HTTP request/response model.

Static Resource Serving

CherryPy provides two simple tools to serve either a single file or an entire directory. In either case CherryPy takes care of the HTTP caching aspect of your static resource by automatically checking the presence of the If-Modified-Since and If-Unmodified-Since headers in the request and returning directly the 304 Not Modified response, if that's the case.

Using the Staticfile Tool to Serve a Single File

The staticfile tool can be used to serve a single file.

Arguments:

Name	Default	Description
filename	N/A	Absolute or relative path to the physical file.
root	None	If filename is relative you must provide the root directory of the file.
match	""	Regular expression to check that the URI path matches a certain pattern.
content_types	None	Dictionary of the form ext: mime type.

Example:

For this purpose let's imagine we have the following directory layout:

```
application \
        myapp.py
        design1.css
```

design1.css is set as follows:

```
body {
    background-color: #86da12;
}
```

The myapp.py module will be defined like this:

```
import cherrypy

class MyApp:
    @cherrypy.expose
    def index(self):
        return """<html>
<head>
  <title>My application</title>
  <link rel="stylesheet" href="css/style.css" type="text/css"></link>
</head>
<html>
<body>
  Hello to you.
</body>
</html>"""

if __name__ == '__main__':
    import os.path
    current_dir = os.path.dirname(os.path.abspath(__file__))
    cherrypy.config.update({'environment': 'production',
                            'log.screen': True})

    conf = {'/': {'tools.staticfile.root': current_dir},
            '/css/style.css': {'tools.staticfile.on': True,
                               'tools.staticfile.filename':
                               'design1.css'}}
    cherrypy.quickstart(MyApp(), '/my', config=conf)
```

Several points must be taken into consideration:

- The root directory can be set globally for the entire application so that you don't have to define it for each URI path.
- When using the staticfile tool the URI and the physical resource need not have the same name. In fact they can be entirely unrelated in their naming as in the previous example.

- Note also that even though the application is mounted on the /my prefix, meaning that requests to the CSS file will be /my/css/style.css (note that this is the case because the path provided in the href attribute of the link element is relative and not absolute: it does not start with a /), our configuration settings do not include the prefix. As we have seen in Chapter 3, this is because the configuration settings are independent from where the application is mounted.

Using the Staticdir Tool to Serve a Complete Directory

The staticdir tool can be used to serve a complete directory.

Arguments:

Name	Default	Description
dir	N/A	Absolute or relative path to the physical directory.
root	None	If dir is relative you must provide the root directory of the file.
match	""	Regular expression pattern to match files.
content_types	None	Dictionary of the form ext: mime type.
index	""	If the URI is not directed at a file but at a directory, you can specify the name of the physical index file to be served.

Example:

Consider the new directory layout.

```
application \
      myapp.py
      data \
        design1.css
        some.js
      feeds \
        app.rss
        app.atom
```

Handling that structure via the static directory tool would be similar to:

```python
import cherrypy

class MyApp:
    @cherrypy.expose
    def index(self):
        return """<html>
<head>
  <title>My application</title>
  <link rel="stylesheet" href="static/css/design1.css"
  type="text/css"></link>
  <script type="application/javascript"
  src="static/scripts/some.js"></script>
</head>
<html>
<body>
  <a href="feed/app.rss">RSS 2.0 feed</a>
  <a href="feed/app.atom">Atom 1.0 feed</a>
</body>
</html>"""

if __name__ == '__main__':
    import os.path
    current_dir = os.path.dirname(os.path.abspath(__file__))
    cherrypy.config.update({'environment': 'production',
                            'log.screen': True})

    conf = {'/': {'tools.staticdir.root': current_dir},
            '/static/css': {'tools.gzip.on': True,
                            'tools.gzip.mime_types':['text/css'],
                            'tools.staticdir.on': True,
                            'tools.staticdir.dir': 'data'},
            '/static/scripts': {'tools.gzip.on': True,
                                'tools.gzip.mime_types':
                                ['application/javascript'],
                                'tools.staticdir.on': True,
                                'tools.staticdir.dir': 'data'},
            '/feed': {'tools.staticdir.on': True,
                      'tools.staticdir.dir': 'feeds',
                      'tools.staticdir.content_types':
                          {'rss':'application/xml',
                           'atom': 'application/atom+xml'}}}
    cherrypy.quickstart(MyApp(), '/', config=conf)
```

In this example, you will note that the URI paths for the CSS and the JavaScript files match exactly their physical counterparts. Also take a close look at how we define the appropriate `Content-Type` for the resource based on the file extension. This is useful when CherryPy cannot determine the proper MIME type to be used on its own. Finally, see how we mix the static directory tool with the `gzip` one so that our static content is compressed before being served.

You may find it limiting that CherryPy requires absolute paths to work with the different static tools. But consider the fact that CherryPy cannot control how an application will be deployed and where it will live. Therefore, it is up to the deployers to provide that information. Remember, however, that the absolute path can be provided via the `root` attribute or directly within the `filename` or `dir` ones.

Bypassing Static Tools to Serve Static Content

Sometimes you may want to reuse CherryPy's internal functionalities for serving content but without using the static tools directly. This is possible by calling the `serve_file` function from your page handler. This function is actually the one called by the built-in tools as well. Consider the following example:

```python
import os.path
import cherrypy
from cherrypy.lib.static import serve_file

class Root:
    @cherrypy.expose
    def feed(self, name):
        accepts = cherrypy.request.headers.elements('Accept')

        for accept in accepts:
            if accept.value == 'application/atom+xml':
                return serve_file(os.path.join(current_dir, 'feeds',
                                               '%s.atom' % name),
                                  content_type='application/atom+xml')

        # Not Atom accepted? Well then send RSS instead...
        return serve_file(os.path.join(current_dir, 'feeds',
                                       '%s.rss' % name),
                          content_type='application/xml')
```

```
if __name__ == '__main__':
    current_dir = os.path.dirname(os.path.abspath(__file__))
    cherrypy.config.update({'environment': 'production',
                            'log.screen': True})
    cherrypy.quickstart(Root(), '/')
```

Here we define a feed page handler that, when called, will check what is the preferred representation of the feed of the user-agent—it maybe RSS or Atom.

WSGI Support

Web Server Gateway Interface (WSGI) is defined in a **Python Enhancement Proposal (PEP-333)** written by Phillip J. Eby to provide a loosely-coupled bridge between the web server and web applications.

WSGI defines the following three components:

- Server or gateway
- Middleware
- Application or framework

The following figure shows WSGI along with its layers:

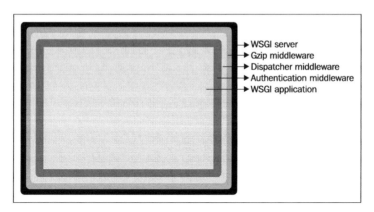

The goal of WSGI is to allow components to be plugged and played at will, with the minimum API overhead possible. This allows code reuse of common functionalities such as session, authentication, URL dispatching, logging, etc. In fact, because the API is minimal and unobtrusive, frameworks or libraries supporting the WSGI specification will be able to handle these components.

Until CherryPy 3.0, the support of WSGI within CherryPy was not welcome due to the internal design of CherryPy and also the belief that WSGI would not necessarily make the product a better one. When Robert Brewer undertook the refactoring of the project, he improved the WSGI support based on the work achieved by Christian Wyglendowski to the point of making it a first class citizen within CherryPy and therefore fulfilling expectations from the community.

> Note that CherryPy tools and WSGI middlewares are different by design but not by capability. They aim at providing the same functionalities in a distinct way. CherryPy tools are mainly meaningful within CherryPy and are therefore optimized in that context. CherryPy tools and WSGI middlewares can coexist in a single application.

Hosting a WSGI Application within the CherryPy WSGI Server

Let's see an example on how to use CherryPy in a WSGI environment:

```python
import cherrypy
from paste.translogger import TransLogger

def application(environ, start_response):
    status = '200 OK'
    response_headers = [('Content-type', 'text/plain')]
    start_response(status, response_headers)
    return ['Hello world!\n']

if __name__ == '__main__':
    cherrypy.tree.graft(TransLogger(application), script_name='/')
    cherrypy.server.quickstart()
    cherrypy.engine.start()
```

Let's explain what we have done:

1. First we create a WSGI application respecting the WSGI specification, hence a Python callable respecting the WSGI application signature. The `environ` parameter contains values to be propagated orthogonally across the processing from the server to the application. Middlewares can alter this dictionary by adding new values or transforming existing values. The `start_response` parameter is a Python callable provided by the outer layer (a middleware or ultimately the WSGI server) to perform the response processing. Our WSGI application then returns an iterable, which will be consumed by the outer layers.

2. Then, we encapsulate the application into a middleware provided by the paste package. Paste is a suite of common WSGI middlewares created and maintained by Ian Bicking. In our example, we use the `TransLogger` middleware to enable logging of incoming requests. WSGI defines middlewares to act like a server for encapsulated WSGI applications and as an application for the hosting WSGI server.

3. Finally, we graft the WSGI application into the CherryPy tree through the `cherrypy.tree.graft()` method and we start the CherryPy server and engine.

As the built-in CherryPy server is a WSGI server, it can handle the WSGI application without any trouble. Bear in mind, however, that many aspects of CherryPy such as tools and configuration settings will not be applied to the hosted WSGI application. You will need to use middlewares to perform operations such as the `paste.transLogger`. Alternatively, you can use the `wsgiapp` tool as follows:

```python
import cherrypy
from paste.translogger import TransLogger

def application(environ, start_response):
    status = '200 OK'
    response_headers = [('Content-type', 'text/plain')]
    start_response(status, response_headers)
    return ['Hello world!\n']

class Root:
    pass

if __name__ == '__main__':
    app = TransLogger(application)
    conf = {'/': {'tools.wsgiapp.on': True,
                  'tools.wsgiapp.app': app,
                  'tools.gzip.on': True}}
```

```
cherrypy.tree.mount(Root(), '/', config=conf)
cherrypy.server.quickstart()
cherrypy.engine.start()
```

In this example, we wrap the WSGI application using the `wsgiapp` tool. Notice that we can apply tools on the WSGI application as if it was a regular page handler.

Hosting a CherryPy WSGI Application within a Third-Party WSGI Server

In this example, we will write a CherryPy application as we traditionally do and host it in a WSGI server different from the built-in one. Indeed, we will be using the default WSGI server provided by the `wsgiref` package.

 The `wsgiref` package is a set of WSGI helpers that has become part of the Python standard library as of Python 2.5. Otherwise, you can get it via `easy_install wsgiref`.

```
import cherrypy
from cherrypy import tools
from wsgiref.simple_server import make_server
from flup.middleware.gzip import GzipMiddleware

class Root:
    @cherrypy.expose
    @tools.response_headers(headers=[('Content-Language', 'en-GB')])
    def index(self):
        return "Hello world!"

if __name__ == '__main__':
    wsgi_app = cherrypy.Application(Root(), script_name="/")
    cherrypy.engine.start(blocking=False)

    httpd = make_server('localhost', 8080, GzipMiddleware(wsgi_app))
    print "HTTP Serving HTTP on http://localhost:8080/"
    httpd.serve_forever()
```

Let's explain this example:

1. First we create a regular CherryPy application. Note how we can still safely use CherryPy tools in this context.

2. Then we make a WSGI application from it through the `cherrypy.Application` helper. This returns a WSGI-valid callable made of the CherryPy application.

3. Next we start the CherryPy engine in a non-blocking mode as we still need CherryPy to handle the request and dispatch to the correct page handler.

4. Then we create a WSGI server instance hosting our WSGI application, which is encapsulated in the gzip middleware, which compresses the response body. This middleware is provided by the `flup` package, which is another WSGI set of middlewares. (Flup is maintained by Allan Saddi.)

To conclude, the level of support for WSGI within CherryPy 3 is excellent, while being flexible enough so that you can use the best of both designs when need be. CherryPy can be seen as a comprehensive and coherent WSGI implementation. Moreover, CherryPy has the most comprehensive and fastest WSGI server currently available and you have no reason to believe you should drop the library if you want WSGI support. You can get more information about WSGI at `http://wsgi.org`.

Summary

In this chapter, we have reviewed key points of the CherryPy library, which will hopefully open your mind on how to make the most of its capabilities. While being a small package CherryPy offers an extended and yet coherent set of features all geared towards making your life easier. Some aspects of CherryPy have been left out, however, as they go beyond the scope of this book and the best place to gather more detailed information is by visiting the user and developer public mailing lists.

Now that you have acquired a good background with the library, we will move on to using it by developing a simple photoblog application.

A Photoblog Application

5

In this chapter, we are going to explain what the next few chapters will put in place to develop a photoblog application. In the first half of this chapter, we will review the goals and features of this application from a high-level perspective without going into too much detail. In the second half, we will define the entities that our application will manipulate and introduce the concept of object-relational mappers, which aim at reducing the impedance mismatch between relational database and object-oriented software design. We will briefly present the most common Python ORMs and then develop our application data access layer based on the Dejavu ORM.

A Photoblog Application

In the previous chapters, we have reviewed CherryPy's design and features in detail but we haven't demonstrated its use in the context of a web application. The next few chapters will undertake this task by going through the development of a photoblog application.

A photoblog is like a regular blog except that the principal content is not text but photographs. The main reason for choosing a photoblog is that the range of features to be implemented is small enough so that we can concentrate on their design and implementation.

The goals behind going through this application are as follows:

- To see how to slice the development of a web application into meaningful layers and therefore show that a web application is not very different from a rich application sitting on your desktop.
- To show that the separation of concerns can also be applied to the web interface itself by using principles grouped under the name of Ajax.
- To introduce common Python packages for dealing with common aspects of web development such as database access, HTML templating, JavaScript handling, etc.

Photoblog Entities

As mentioned earlier, the photoblog will try to stay as simple as possible in order to focus on the other aspects of developing a web application. In this section, we will briefly describe the entities our photoblog will manipulate as well as their attributes and relations with each other.

In a nutshell our photoblog application will use the following entities and they will be associated as shown in the following figure:

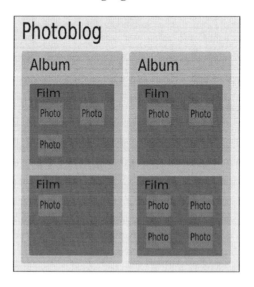

This figure is not what our application will look like but it shows the entities our application will manipulate. One photoblog will contain several albums, which in turn will host as many films as required, which will carry the photographs.

In other words, we will design our application with the following entity structure:

Entity: Photoblog

Role: This entity will be the root of the application.

Attributes:

- `name`: A unique identifier for the blog
- `title`: A public label for the blog

Relations:

- One photoblog will have zero to many albums

Entity: Album

Role: An album carries a story told by the photographs as an envelope.

Attributes:

- `name`: A unique identifier for the album
- `title`: A public label for the album
- `author`: The name of the album's author
- `description`: A simple description of the album used in feeds
- `story`: A story attached to the album
- `created`: A timestamp of when the album is being created
- `modified`: A timestamp of when the album is being modified
- `blog_id`: A reference to the blog handling the album

Relations:

- One album will reference zero to several films

Entity: Film

Role: A film gathers a set of photographs.

Attributes:

- `name`: A unique identifier for the film
- `title`: A public label for the film
- `created`: A timestamp of when the film is being created
- `modified`: A timestamp of when the film is being modified
- `album_id`: A reference to the album

Relations:

- A film will reference zero to several photographs

Entity: Photo

Role: The unit of our application is a photograph.

Attributes:

- `name`: A unique identifier for the photo
- `legend`: A legend associated with the photograph
- `filename`: The base name of the photograph on the hard-disk
- `filesize`: The size in bytes of the photograph
- `width`: Width of the photograph in pixels
- `height`: Height of the photograph in pixels
- `created`: A timestamp of when the photograph is being created
- `modified`: A timestamp of when the photograph is being modified
- `film_id`: A reference to the film carrying the photograph

Relations: None

Functionally, the photoblog application will provide APIs to manipulate those entities via the traditional **CRUD** interface: **Create**, **Retrieve**, **Update**, and **Delete**. We will elaborate more on this in Chapter 6.

Now that we have briefly introduced what kind of application we will be developing throughout the following chapters we can move on to the next section and start reviewing our options to handle the database aspect of the application. But first a quick glossary of the terms this chapter will use.

Vocabulary

Here is a list of the terms we will be using:

- Persistence: Persistence is the concept of data items outliving the execution of programs manipulating them. Simply put, it is the process of storing data in long lasting memory medium such as a disk.
- Database: A database is a collection of organized data. There are different organization models: hierarchical, network, relational, object-oriented, etc. A database holds the logical representation of its data.
- Database Management System (DBMS): A DBMS is a group of related software applications to manipulate data in a database. A DBMS platform should offer the following among other features:
    - Persistence of the data
    - A query language to manipulate data
    - Concurrency control

- ° Security control
- ° Integrity control
- ° Transaction capabilities

We will use **DBMSes** as the plural of DBMS.

DBMSes Overview

In this section, we will quickly review the different kinds of existing DBMSes. The goal is to quickly introduce their main characteristics.

Relational Database Management System (RDBMS)

Of all DBMSes, the RDBMS is the most common, whether it is in small applications or multi-national infrastructure. An RDBMS comes with a database based on the concepts of the relational model, a mathematical model that permits the logical representation of a collection of data through relations. A relational database should be a concrete implementation of the relational model. However, modern relational databases follow the model only to a certain degree.

The following table shows the correlation between the terms of the relational model and the relational database implementation.

Relational Model	Relational Database
Relation	Table
Attribute	Column
Tuple	Row

Relational databases support a set of types to define the domain of scope a column can use. However, there are only a limited number of supported types, which can be an issue with complex data types as allowed in objected-oriented design.

Structure Query Language more commonly known as **SQL** is the language used to define, manipulate, or control data within a relational database.

The following table is a quick summary of SQL keywords and their contexts.

Context	Keywords
Data manipulation	SELECT, INSERT, UPDATE, DELETE
Data definition	CREATE, DROP, ALTER
Data control	GRANT, REVOKE
Transaction	START, COMMIT, ROLLBACK

A construction of these keywords is called an SQL statement. When executed, an SQL statement returns a collection of rows of the data matching the query or nothing.

The relational model algebra uses the relation composition to compose operations across different sets; this is translated in the relational database context by **joins**. Joining tables allows complex queries to be shaped to filter out data.

SQL provides the following three kinds of joins:

Union Type	Description
INNER JOIN	Intersection between two tables.
LEFT OUTER JOIN	Limits the result set by the left table. So all results from the left table will be returned with their matching result in the right table. If no matching result is found, it will return a NULL value.
RIGHT OUTER JOIN	Same as the LEFT OUTER JOIN except that the tables are reversed.

There is no RDBMS written in Python but most RDBMSes can be accessed via a corresponding Python library.

Object-Oriented Database Management System (OODBMS)

An OODBMS uses the object-oriented model to organize and store information. In other words, an OODBMS allows objects to be stored without having to be mapped into a different data structure like the relational database. This implies a great consistency between the database persisting the data and the application layers encapsulating it. In fact, the persistence mechanism is unobtrusive to the developer.

XML Database Management System (XMLDBMS)

Native XML Databases (**NXDs**) use XML documents as the unit of data they store and manipulate. XMLDBMSes on top of NXDs are optimized in this sense and provide native support for standard XML selection and querying languages such as XPath and XQuery. Some modern RDBMSes offer XML support through transparent conversion between the XML and relational data model leveraging the introduction of an XML database requirement.

Object-Relational Mapping

For the last fifteen years the software industry has moved towards a generalized use of the object-oriented modeling paradigm in the different layers of software application development. One of the last bastions that have resisted against this wave has been the database domain. Nonetheless, over the years quite an important amount of work has been conducted with success in order to develop OODBMSes for filling the gap of managing data. In spite of that OODBMSes have not taken off enough to steal RDBMS's thunder.

There are several factors behind this:

- Cost of changing the market. For decades RDBMSes have been the DBMSes of predilection to store and organize data. Most businesses have built their infrastructure around RDBMSes and changing that state is an immense task and only few are ready to pay for such a risk.

- Cost of migrating existing data. Even if a company is ready to step into that direction for new projects, it is unlikely it will for the existing infrastructure as the cost of migration and integration would be too high.

- Lack of unified query language.

- Lack of third-party software such as reporting tools based on OODBMS.

- Lack of experts. Finding a database administrator for a RDBMS is much easier than for an ODBMS.

Object-Relational Mappers (**ORMs**) succeeded because they were an efficient and cost-effective answer to some of the enumerated issues. The principle behind object-relational mapping is to reduce the impedance mismatch between the two models with minimum intrusion. ORMs allow the database designer and administrator to keep their beloved RDBMSes while proposing an objected-oriented interface to a certain extent to the software developer. ORM is an extra layer between the database and the application which translates an object into a database row and vice versa.

It is important to bear in mind though that ORM can alleviate the problem only to a certain degree and that in some cases the differences between the relational and object design cannot be met without some compromise on both sides. For example, most ORMs correlate a database table into a class, which works fine when the number of entities and their relationships stay at a basic level. Unfortunately, this one-to-one relationship between a table and a class does not always work well in more complex object-oriented design. In such cases the impedance mismatch between the relational and object-oriented models may force designers to make concessions that could have negative impacts in the long run in regards to extending and maintaining the software.

Python Object-Relational Mappers

This section will introduce three ORMs in a very basic example in order to provide a basic understanding of how they work and their differences. The purpose is not to declare one of these ORMs the winner but to give you an idea of their design and features.

The three ORMs we will cover are:

- SQLObject from Ian Bicking
- SQLAlchemy from Michael Bayer
- Dejavu from Robert Brewer

Although great care has been taken in this section, it may happen that by the time you read this chapter these products might have changed a bit. You will have to refer to their official documentation.

In the following example we will map the following entities:

- Artist: An artist is made of a name. An artist can have zero or several albums.
- Album: An album is made of a title and a release year. An album is associated to an artist and can have zero or more songs.
- Song: A song is made of a name and a position within the album. A song is associated to an album.

This example should be seen as a stripped down version of our photoblog entity set that we defined at the start of this chapter in order to focus on the actual features of each ORM rather than on the entities themselves.

Step 1: **Mapping the entities**

SQLObject

```
from sqlobject import *

class Song(SQLObject):
    title = StringCol()
    position = IntCol()
    album = ForeignKey('Album', cascade=True)

class Album(SQLObject):
    title = StringCol()
    release_year = IntCol()
    artist = ForeignKey('Artist', cascade=True)
    songs = MultipleJoin('Song', orderBy="position")

class Artist(SQLObject):
    # Using alternateID will automatically
    # create a byName() method
    name = StringCol(alternateID=True, unique=True)
    albums = MultipleJoin('Album')
```

The first point to note is that SQLObject does not require a separate declaration of the mapping that is done within the class itself. Each class must inherit from the unobtrusive `SQLObject` class to be manageable by SQLObject and the attributes will be mapped transparently by SQLObject into the table's columns. SQLObject automatically adds an attribute `id` to hold the unique identifier of each object. This means that every table mapped by SQLObject must have a primary key.

`ForeignKey` or `MultipleJoin` are examples of how to define the relationships between entities. Note that they need the name of the class as a string and not the class object itself. This allows the declaration of relationships without the prior existence of each class within the scope of the module. In other words `Artist` and `Album` could be declared in two different modules without the problem of cross imports.

SQLObject offers a useful feature when specifying `alternateID` as a parameter in one of the class attributes. By using it, SQLObject adds a new method to the class of the form `byAttributeName` as shown in the example above. Note also how you can specify at that level the way rows must be ordered when being retrieved.

Finally bear in mind that by default SQLObject auto-commits to the database each modification made to an attribute, which can increase the network overhead as well as break the database integrity if an error occurs. To work around this behavior SQLObject offers the `set` method on an SQLObject object that performs one single UPDATE query for all the modifications limiting the required bandwidth. Moreover, SQLObject supports the concept of transactions, allowing us to ensure that operations are atomic to the database and can then be rolled back if an error occurs. Note that the transactions have to be explicitly requested by the developer.

SQLAlchemy

```
from sqlalchemy import *

artist_table = Table('Artist', metadata,
                    Column('id', Integer, primary_key=True),
                    Column('name', String(), unique=True))

song_table = Table('Song', metadata,
                    Column('id', Integer, primary_key=True),
                    Column('title', String()),
                    Column('position', Integer),
                    Column('album_id', Integer,
                        ForeignKey('Album.id')))

album_table = Table('Album', metadata,
                    Column('id', Integer, primary_key=True),
                    Column('title', String()),
                    Column('release_year', Integer),
                    Column('artist_id', Integer,
                        ForeignKey('Artist.id')))

class Artist(object):
    def __init__(self, name):
        self.id = None
        self.name = name

class Album(object):
    def __init__(self, title, release_year=0):
        self.id = None
        self.title = title
        self.release_year = release_year

class Song(object):
    def __init__(self, title, position=0):
        self.id = None
```

```
        self.title = title
        self.position = position

song_mapper = mapper(Song, song_table)
album_mapper = mapper(Album, album_table,
                      properties = {'songs': relation(song_mapper,
                                     cascade="all, delete-orphan")
                                   })
artist_mapper = mapper(Artist, artist_table,
                       properties = {'albums': relation(album_mapper,
                                      cascade="all, delete-orphan")
                                    })
```

SQLAlchemy uses a declarative mapping style as you can see. The first step is to express tables into their Python syntax counterpart. Then we need to declare the class our application will manipulate. Note how they don't need to inherit from an SQLAlchemy class even though they must inherit from the built-in Python object class. Eventually, we map both aspects through the `mapper` function, which also allows us to inform SQLAlchemy of the relationships between entities.

You will notice how the identifier of each table is explicitly declared unlike SQLObject and Dejavu. Similarly you do not specify at that level how fetched rows must be ordered as this will be specified at the query level.

Dejavu

```
from dejavu import Unit, UnitProperty

class Song(Unit):
    title = UnitProperty(unicode)
    position = UnitProperty(int)
    album_id = UnitProperty(int, index=True)

class Album(Unit):
    title = UnitProperty(unicode)
    release_year = UnitProperty(int)
    artist_id = UnitProperty(int, index=True)

    def songs(self):
        return self.Song()
    songs = property(songs)

    def artist(self):
        return self.Artist()
    artist = property(artist)
```

```
        def on_forget(self):
            for song in self.Song():
                song.forget()

    class Artist(Unit):
        name = UnitProperty(unicode)

        def albums(self):
            return self.Album()
        albums = property(albums)



        def on_forget(self):
            for album in self.Album():
                album.forget()

    Album.one_to_many('ID', Song, 'album_id')
    Artist.one_to_many('ID', Album, 'artist_id')
```

Like SQLObject, Dejavu does lots of work under the hood. Each class participating in the mapping must inherit from Unit. The attributes of the class represent the columns of the table. Only the relationship between the entities is done through a more declarative interface.

One difference between Dejavu and the other two is that it does not provide the cascade delete feature. This means that this has to be accomplished from the class itself by defining an on_forget() method and specifying what tasks should be done when deleting a unit. This might look at first sight like a drawback but offers, in fact, a fine granularity on how you propagate a cascade delete.

Step 2: **Setting up the access to the database**

SQLObject

```
    # Create a connection to a SQLlite 'in memory' database
    sqlhub.processConnection =
    connectionForURI('sqlite:/:memory:?debug=True')
```

SQLAlchemy

```
    # Inform SQLAlchemy of the database we will use
    # A SQLlite 'in memory' database
    # Mapped into an engine object and bound to a high
    # level meta data interface
    engine = create_engine('sqlite:///:memory:', echo=True)
    metadata = BoundMetaData(engine)
```

Dejavu

```
# Create the global arena object
arena = dejavu.Arena()
arena.logflags = dejavu.logflags.SQL + dejavu.logflags.IO

# Add a storage to the main arena object

conf = {'Database': ":memory:"}
arena.add_store("main","sqlite", conf)

# Register units the arena will be allowed to handle
# This call must happen after the declaration of the units
# and those must be part of the current namespace
arena.register_all(globals())
```

Step 3: **Manipulating tables**

SQLObject

```
def create_tables():
    Album.createTable()
    Song.createTable()
    Artist.createTable()

def drop_tables():
    Song.dropTable()
    Artist.dropTable()
    Album.dropTable()
```

SQLAlchemy

```
def create_tables():
    artist_table.create(checkfirst=True)
    album_table.create(checkfirst=True)
    song_table.create(checkfirst=True)

def drop_tables():
    artist_table.drop(checkfirst=False)
    song_table.drop(checkfirst=False)
    album_table.drop(checkfirst=False)
```

Dejavu

```
def create_tables():
    arena.create_storage(Song)
    arena.create_storage(Album)
    arena.create_storage(Artist)
```

```
def drop_tables():
    arena.drop_storage(Song)
    arena.drop_storage(Album)
    arena.drop_storage(Artist)
```

Step 4: **Loading data**

SQLObject

```
# Create an artist
jeff_buckley = Artist(name="Jeff Buckley")

# Create an album for that artist
grace = Album(title="Grace", artist=jeff_buckley, release_year=1994)

# Add songs to that album
dream_brother = Song(title="Dream Brother", position=10, album=grace)
mojo_pin = Song(title="Mojo Pin", position=1, album=grace)
lilac_wine = Song(title="Lilac Wine", position=4, album=grace)
```

SQLAlchemy

```
session = create_session(bind_to=engine)

jeff_buckley = Artist(name="Jeff Buckley")

grace = Album(title="Grace", release_year=1994)

dream_brother = Song(title="Dream Brother", position=10)
mojo_pin = Song(title="Mojo Pin", position=1)
lilac_wine = Song(title="Lilac Wine", position=4)

grace.songs.append(dream_brother)
grace.songs.append(mojo_pin)
grace.songs.append(lilac_wine)
jeff_buckley.albums.append(grace)
session.save(jeff_buckley)
session.flush()
```

Note the fact that each object is created independently from the other and their relationship is fulfilled in a second step, e.g. the append() method on the grace.songs object.

In the same declarative spirit as above SQLAlchemy does not commit automatically by default to the database. Instead it delays the operation until you flush the current session of work.

Dejavu

```
sandbox = arena.new_sandbox()

# Create an artist unit
jeff_buckley = Artist(name="Jeff Buckley")
sandbox.memorize(jeff_buckley)

grace = Album(title="Grace", release_year=1994)
sandbox.memorize(grace)

# Add the album unit to the artist unit
jeff_buckley.add(grace)

dream_brother = Song(title="Dream Brother", position=10)
sandbox.memorize(dream_brother)

mojo_pin = Song(title="Mojo Pin", position=1)
sandbox.memorize(mojo_pin)

lilac_wine = Song(title="Lilac Wine", position=4)
sandbox.memorize(lilac_wine)

# Add each song unit to the album unit
grace.add(dream_brother)
grace.add(mojo_pin)
grace.add(lilac_wine)

sandbox.flush_all()
```

Dejavu provides the concept of sandboxes in which you can isolate the entities you manipulate. Also note that newly created units do not exist for their relatives until you call the `sandbox.memorize()` method, which puts the unit into the sandbox.

Like SQLAlchemy, Dejavu delays the commit operation until you explicitly call the `sandbox.flush_all()` method.

Step 5: **Manipulating data**

First we define a function that will take an artist and display the albums' songs.

```
def display_info(artist):
    for album in artist.albums:
        message = """
%s released %s in %d
It contains the following songs:\n""" % (artist.name,
                                         album.title,
                                         album.release_year)
```

```
        for song in album.songs:
            message = message + "          %s\n" % (song.title, )
        print message
```

SQLObject

```python
# Retrieve an artist by his name
buckley = Artist.byName('Jeff Buckley')
display_info(buckley)

# Retrieve songs containing the word 'la' from the given artist
# The AND() function is provided by the SQLObject namespace
songs = Song.select(AND(Artist.q.name=="Jeff Buckley",
                        Song.q.title.contains("la")))
for song in songs:
    print "  %s" % (song.title,)

# Retrieve all songs but only display some of them
songs = Song.select()
print "Found %d songs, let's show only a few of them:" %
(songs.count(), )
for song in songs[1:-1]:
    print "  %s" % (song.title,)

# Retrieve an album by its ID
album = Album.get(1)
print album.title

# Delete the album and all its dependencies
# since we have specified cascade delete
album.destroySelf()
```

SQLAlchemy

```python
session = create_session(bind_to=engine)

# Retrieve an artist by his name
buckley = session.query(Artist).get_by(name='Jeff Buckley')
display_info(buckley)

# Retrieve songs containing the word 'la' from the given artist
songs = session.query(Song).select(and_(artist_table.c.name=="Jeff
                                         Buckley",
                                         song_table.c.title.like
                                         ("%la%")))
```

```
for song in songs:
    print "  %s" % (song.title,)

# Retrieve all songs but only display some of them
# Note that we specify the order by clause at this level
songs = session.query(Song).select(order_by=[Song.c.position])
print "Found %d songs, let's show only a few of them:" % (len(songs),)
for song in songs[1:-1]:
    print "  %s" % (song.title,)

# Retrieve an album by its ID
album = session.query(Album).get_by(id=1)
print album.title

# Delete the album and all its dependencies
# since we have specified cascade delete
session.delete(album)
session.flush()
```

Dejavu

```
sandbox = arena.new_sandbox()

# Retrieve an artist by his name
buckley = sandbox.Artist(name="Jeff Buckley")
display_info(buckley)

# Retrieve songs containing the word 'la' from the given artist
# We will explain in more details the concepts of Expressions
f = lambda ar, al, s: ar.name == "Jeff Buckley" and "la" in s.title

# Note how we express the composition between the units
results = sandbox.recall(Artist & Album & Song, f)
for artist, album, song in results:
    print "  %s" % (song.title,)

# Retrieve all songs but only display some of them
songs = sandbox.recall(Song)
print "Found %d songs, let's show only a few of them:" % (len(songs),)
for song in songs[1:-1]:
    print "  %s" % (song.title,)

# Retrieve an album by its ID
album = sandbox.Album(ID=1)
print album.title
```

Choosing an object-relational mapper is a difficult task as it is usually after using one for a while that you can really measure the impact it has on the development design and process. As previously stated, it is critical to acknowledge that ORMs do not remove the impedance mismatch between the relational and object-oriented model.

SQLObject has a low-learning curve and quite a big community, which makes it suitable for developers debuting in the use of ORM. The project is aiming at its next version, which will fix a fair number of bad design decisions made in its early life while slowly abandoning the current version.

SQLAlchemy has based its design on the Hibernate ORM from the Java world and has thus avoided lots of pitfalls that SQLObject has not. Its declarative syntax will not please every pythoner but its flexibility and good documentation have placed SQLAlchemy as a very serious candidate in the field.

Dejavu is a fairly unknown ORM and thus has a small community. It is well documented and comes with relevant example cases. Its strength resides in its capacity to move away from the underlying relational database layer by providing a very high-level interface using common Python idioms.

For instance, SQLObject and SQLAlchemy do use terms such as `table`, `column`, or `select` while Dejavu refers to `storage` and `unit` providing a better abstraction to the underlying mechanisms.

This is also true when it comes to the process of building queries. Unlike SQLObject and SQLAlchemy, which stay very close to SQL by providing a Python interface to SQL statements, Dejavu provides an interface independent of SQL. Review the section on manipulating data for an example.

These are the reasons why our photoblog application will use Dejavu instead of SQLObject or SQLAlchemy. However, keep in mind that they are all good and powerful ORMs.

Photoblog Application Entity Modeling

First we define what we will call a `storage` module providing a simple interface to some common operations like the connection to the database.

```
import dejavu
arena = dejavu.Arena()

from model import Photoblog, Album, Film, Photo

def connect():
```

```
conf = {'Connect': "host=localhost dbname=photoblog user=test
        password=test"}
arena.add_store("main", "postgres", conf)

arena.register_all(globals())
```

In this case, we import the dejavu module and we create one global instance of the Arena class. The arena will be our interface between the underlying storage manager and the business logic layer.

The connect function adds a storage manager to the arena object for a PostgreSQL RDBMS and then registers all imported entities so that the arena object knows what entities it will manage. (Please refer to the Dejavu documentation for a list of supported database managers and how to declare them within the add_store() method.) Once we have this module we can start mapping entities.

Mapping Entities

Mapping the entities is done through the following process:

- Creating a class that inherits from Unit
- Adding attributes using the UnitProperty class
- Setting up the relationship between units

Entity: Photoblog

```
from dejavu import Unit, UnitProperty

from engine.database import arena
from album import Album

class Photoblog(Unit):
    name = UnitProperty(unicode)
    title = UnitProperty(unicode)

    def on_forget(self):
        for album in self.Album():
            album.forget()

Photoblog.one_to_many('ID', Album, 'blog_id')
```

Entity: Album

```
import datetime

from dejavu import Unit, UnitProperty
from engine.database import arena
```

```
from film import Film

class Album(Unit):
    name = UnitProperty(unicode)
    title = UnitProperty(unicode)
    author = UnitProperty(unicode)
    description = UnitProperty(unicode)
    content = UnitProperty(unicode, hints={u'bytes': 0})
    created = UnitProperty(datetime.datetime)
    modified = UnitProperty(datetime.datetime)
    blog_id = UnitProperty(int, index=True)

    def on_forget(self):
        for film in self.Film():
            film.forget()

Album.one_to_many('ID', Film, 'album_id')
```

Entity: Film

```
import datetime

from dejavu import Unit, UnitProperty
from engine.database import arena

from photo import Photo

class Film(Unit):
    name = UnitProperty(unicode)
    title = UnitProperty(unicode)
    created = UnitProperty(datetime.datetime)
    modified = UnitProperty(datetime.datetime)
    album_id = UnitProperty(int, index=True)

    def on_forget(self):
        for photo in self.Photo():
            photo.forget()

Film.one_to_many('ID', Photo, 'film_id')
```

Entity: Photo

```
import datetime

from dejavu import Unit, UnitProperty
from engine.database import arena
```

```
class Photo(Unit):
    name = UnitProperty(unicode)
    legend = UnitProperty(unicode)
    filename = UnitProperty(unicode)
    filesize = UnitProperty(int)
    width = UnitProperty(int)
    height = UnitProperty(int)

    created = UnitProperty(datetime.datetime)
    modified = UnitProperty(datetime.datetime)
    film_id = UnitProperty(int, index=True)
```

Units and UnitProperties

In the previous section, we mapped our entities into units that Dejavu will manage. All our classes inherit from the Unit base class. This class does not provide much apart from automatically adding an ID property to the class, which is the reason why we do not explicitly provide one in any of our units. Nonetheless by inheriting from the Unit class you allow Dejavu to register and handle your class.

The next step is obviously to add properties to your classes via the UnitProperty class, which has the following signature:

```
UnitProperty(type=unicode, index=False,
             hints=None, key=None, default=None)
```

- The type parameter is a Python type. Dejavu takes care of translating it into the appropriate SQL equivalent type transparently.
- The index parameter indicates whether the column should be indexed by the RDBMS if it supports it.
- The hints parameter is a dictionary to help Dejavu storage managers to optimize the creation of the column. Dejavu has three built-in hints but you can provide yours if you create your own storage manager:
    - bytes: Indicates the number of bytes to be used for a unicode property, 0 meaning unlimited.
    - scale: Number of digits to the right of the decimal point in a numeric column.
    - precision: Total number of digits in a numeric column.
- The key parameter is the property canonical name.
- The default parameter indicates the default value to be used.

Properties will map into the columns of a table in the relational database.

Associating Units

Associating units is the means of giving a shape to your design. Entities are bricks, relations are the mortar.

Dejavu supports the following common relationships:

- One to one (1, 1)
- One to many (1, n)
- Many to one (n, 1)

In each case you provide the signature as follows:

```
nearClass(nearKey, farClass, farKey)
```

Therefore the relation between `Film` and `Photo` is:

```
Film.one_to_many('ID', Photo, 'film_id')
```

The `nearClass` is `Film`, the `nearKey` is `ID` (property of the `nearClass`), the `farClass` is `Photo`, and the `farKey` is `film_id` (property of the `farClass`).

Dejavu does not provide a native many-to-many relationship but this is achievable through a third unit class and a one-to-one relationship.

The Sandbox Interface

The `sandbox` object manages memory dedicated to units in a protected way. A `sandbox` is where units spend their life. There are two ways to create `sandboxes`:

```
box = arena.create_sandbox()
box = dejavu.Sandbox(arena)
```

The former version is the most common and is the one we will use throughout this book.

Let's review a few key methods of the `sandbox` interface:

- `memorize`: When you create a new instance of a unit, it exists only in memory and is separated from the storage manager. You need to call the `memorize` method to make it part of the `sandbox`. This will also set the `ID` of the unit. Additionally this will reserve a place in the underlying database by issuing an `INSERT INTO` SQL statement.

- `forget`: In order to tell the store manager to stop managing a unit you must call the `forget` method. This will delete it from the `sandbox` and from the storage manager.

- repress: In some cases you may wish to clear the unit from the sandbox but not from the store manager. In such cases you should use the repress method.

- recall, xrecall: These two methods allow you to retrieve units based on filters (as we will explain in the section *Querying Units*). The difference between recall and xrecall is that the latter yields results in an iterating fashion whereas the former loads everything into a list at once.

- unit: Both the previous methods are powerful ones to retrieve a set of data but they can be heavy when you simply look for one unit based on a value of its properties. This is what the unit method provides.

- flush_all: Once you have manipulated your units you have to call flush_all in order to make those changes to the physical back end.

As you can see, the interface provided by the Sandbox class is quite simple, straightforward, and yet powerful as the next section will demonstrate.

Querying Units

We have seen so far how to map our entities into units as well as how to manipulate those units. This section will explain in detail how to query the storage manager for units based on criteria.

Within Dejavu querying is done through an Expression instance. The Expression class is a filter for units. Let's take an example to explain how this works.

```
# Search for all photographs with a width superior to 300 pixels

f = lambda x: x.width > 300

box.recall(Photo, f)
```

The first step is to create a function that returns a bool. That function is usually a lambda as there is no need to pollute the Python namespace with meaningless names. Then we pass it to one of the sandbox methods such as recall or xrecall, which will create a logic.Expression instance and apply it.

Expressions show their value when filtering against complex queries such as the one involving JOIN. For example, if you want to join between units you would use Python operators between the units themselves.

```
# Search for all photographs of width superior to 300 pixels
# within albums created by Sylvain
box.recall(Album & Photo, lambda a,
           p: a.author == "Sylvain" and p.width > 300)
```

As you can see, the first parameter of the method takes an aggregation of the unit classes that will take part in the join. Dejavu gives you the opportunity of using Python operators to declare aggregation between units.

When composing between units, the order is important while constructing the `filter` function. In the previous example the `lambda` function parameters will match the order of the composed units. This behavior is mirrored by the result returned by the `recall()` method, which will provide a list of `Album` and `Photo` items.

Below are the Dejavu representations of SQL JOINs.

Join Type	Operator	Description
Inner	& or +	All related pairs of both classes will be returned.
Left Outer	<<	All related pairs of both classes will be returned. In addition, if any Unit in class1 has no match in class2, we return a single row with Unit1 and a **null Unit** (a Unit, all of whose properties are None).
Right Outer	>>	All related pairs of both classes will be returned. In addition, if any Unit in class2 has no match in class1, we return a single row with a null Unit (a Unit, all of whose properties are None) and Unit2.

There is no limitation from Dejavu regarding the aggregation you build. For instance you can write:

```
(Film << Album) & Photo
```

Extending the Data Access Layer

In the previous sections, we have defined the mapping between our entities and the classes our application will manipulate. As they stand these classes are not very useful; in this section we will see how to extend them to provide more functionalities. To keep this section concise, we will only discuss the `Album` class.

Methods to be added to the Album class:

```
def films(self):
    """Returns all the attached films

        album = Album()
        ...

        for film in album.films:
            ...
```

```
    """
    return self.Film()
films = property(films)


def get_all(cls):
    """Returns all the existing albums

        for album in Album.albums:
            ...

    """
    sandbox = arena.new_sandbox()
    return sandbox.recall(Album)
albums = classmethod(get_all)

def fetch(cls, id):
    """Fetch one album by id"""
    sandbox = arena.new_sandbox()
    return sandbox.unit(Album, ID=int(id))
fetch = classmethod(fetch)

def fetch_range(cls, start, end):
    """Fetch a range of albums which ID falls into the
        specified range.

        # This could return up to 5 albums
        albums = Album.fetch_range(4, 9)
        for album in albums:
            ...

    """
    sandbox = arena.new_sandbox()

    # dejavu's views change the capacity of dejavu to
    # perform operations on a Unit

    # here we create a view of the Album unit so that only
    # the created and ID properties appear in the
    # result of the view. A view yields values
    # not units unlike recall or xrecall.
    v = list(sandbox.view(Album, ['created', 'ID']))
    v.sort()
    size = len(v)
    if end > size and start >= size:
```

```
            return None
        elif end > size and start < size:
            end = size
        # row[0]  is the 'created' property value
        # row[1] is the 'ID' property value
        targets = [row[1] for row in v[start:end]]
        return sandbox.recall(Album, lambda x: x.ID in targets)
    fetch_range = classmethod(fetch_range)

    def create(self, photoblog, name, title, slug, author, description,
               content):
        """Instanciates the Album,
        adds it to the passed photoblog and
        persists the changes into the database"""

        sandbox = photoblog.sandbox


        self.name = name
        self.title = title
        self.author = author
        self.description = description
        self.content = content
        self.created = datetime.datetime.now().replace(microsecond=0)
        self.modified = album.created
        self.blog_id = photoblog.ID
        sandbox.memorize(self)
        photoblog.add(self)

        sandbox.flush_all()



    def update(self, name, title, slug, author, description, content):
        """Updates the attributes of an album and
        persists the changes into the storage"""

        self.title = title
        self.slug = slug
        self.author = author
        self.description = description
        self.content = content
        self.modified = datetime.datetime.now().replace(microsecond=0)
        self.sandbox.flush_all()
```

```
def delete(self):
    """Delete the album from the storage"""
    self.sandbox.forget(album)



def to_dict(self):
    """Return an album as a Python dictionary"""
    return {'id': self.ID,
            'uuid': self.uuid,
            'title': self.title,
            'author': self.author,
            'description': self.description,
            'content': self.content,
            'created': self.created.strftime("%d %b. %Y, %H:%M"),
            'modified': self.modified.strftime("%d %b. %Y, %H:%M")}

def to_json(self):
    """JSONify an album properties"""
    return simplejson.dumps(self.to_dict())
```

As you can see, the `Album` class now contains enough methods to allow manipulation of `Album` instances. The other photoblog entities share the same idea and will provide similar interfaces.

Summary

This chapter has introduced the backbone of our photoblog application through the description of its entities and how they are mapped in their Python counterparts. Our next chapter will review how to manipulate those entities from our CherryPy handlers to build the external interface of our application.

6
Web Services

In Chapter 5, we defined the data access layer and the entities our application would manipulate. In this chapter, we will explain how we can articulate our photoblog application by using web services as an API to access and operate the entities we have defined. We will introduce the concept of web services based on the REST principles as well as the Atom Publishing Protocol and explain how we can implement them using CherryPy. By the end of this chapter, you should understand how web services can enhance and extend the capacities of your web application while providing a simple entry point for third-party applications.

Traditional Web Development

Most web applications use the same base URI to handle the serving of resources and the manipulation of resources. For instance, it's common to find something such as the following:

URI	Request Body	HTTP Method	Operation
/album/	N/A	GET	Fetch all albums
/album/?id=12	N/A	GET	Fetch the album with the ID 12
/album/edit?id=12	N/A	GET	Return a form to perform an action on a resource
/album/create	title=Friends	POST	Create an album
/album/delete	id=12	POST	Delete the album with the ID 12
/album/update	id=12&title=Family	POST	Update the album with the ID 12

Within an application hosted with CherryPy, this could be translated into:

```
class Album:
    @cherrypy.expose
    def index(self, id=None):
        # returns all albums as HTML or the one
        # requested by the id parameter if provided

    @cherrypy.expose
    def edit(self, id=None):
        # returns an HTML page with a form to perform
        # an action on a resource (create, update, delete)

    @cherrypy.expose
    def create(self, title):
        # create an album with a title
        # returns an HTML page stating the success

    @cherrypy.expose
    def update(self, id, title):
        # update an album with a title
        # returns an HTML page stating the success

    @cherrypy.expose
    def delete(self, id):
        # delete the album with the given id
        # returns an HTML page stating the success
```

Although this methodology is valid, it is not the best choice when it needs to open itself to different kinds of user agents (browser, robot, service, etc.). For instance, imagine we decide to provide a fat client application to manipulate albums. In such a case, the HTML page returned by the page handlers would be useless; XML or JSON data would be more relevant. We may also want to offer part of our application as a service for third-party applications.

One notable example is the service provided by flickr, (http://www.flickr.com/) the online photo-management application, which allows someone to query the flickr service (http://www.flickr.com/services/api/) for their data in many contexts like getting current photos, activities, blog posts, comments, etc. in different formats. Thanks to these web services a large set of third-party applications have grown to extend flickr users' experience from a web application or even from a fat client application.

Separation of Concerns

The issue with the previous design example is the lack of **separation of concerns**. As Tim Bray said about the Web (please refer to `http://www.tbray.org/ongoing/When/200x/2006/03/26/On-REST` for more details):

You have a lot of things in the system, identified by URIs.

There are two kinds of operations against a resource in the system: those that can change its state, and those that can't.

From the first statement we put a *name* on anything that can pass through the system; we call it a resource. Examples of resources could be a picture, a poem, results of a basketball game, temperature in Australia, etc. We also learn that each resource should be identified in a non-equivocal way. From Tim's second statement we realize that we should logically separate in our design — operations that are read-only and those that can change the resource.

An important corollary of these distinctions is that we would like to let the client inform the server about the content type that it would prefer to receive. In our example, our page handlers solely return HTML pages while it would be more flexible to check what the client can handle and send it the best representation of the resource.

Web application developers should consider the following principles:

- Anything is a resource.
- A resource has one or several identifiers but one identifier can lead to only one resource.
- A resource has one or many representations that the client can request.
- Operations on resources are divided into those that alter the state of the resource and those that do not.

Based on these elements we can redefine our design as follows:

```
class Album:
    @cherrypy.expose
    def index(self):
        # returns all albums as HTML

    @cherrypy.expose
    def default(self, id):
        # returns the album specified or raise a NotFound

    @cherrypy.expose
```

```
        def edit(self, id=None):
            # returns an HTML page with a form to perform
            # an action on a resource (create, update, delete)

    class AlbumManager:
        @cherrypy.expose
        def create(self, title):
            # create an album with a title
            # returns an XML/JSon/XHTML document
            # representing the resource

        @cherrypy.expose
        def update(self, id, title):
            # update an album with a title
            # returns an XML/JSon/XHTML document
            # representing the resource

        @cherrypy.expose
        def delete(self, id):
            # delete the album with the given id
            # returns nothing
```

By doing so we allow any kind of user agent to manipulate a resource by requesting the `AlbumManager` exposed handlers. A browser would still fetch an HTML representation of an album from the `Album` page handlers. You might argue that a browser would not know what is to be done with the returned XML or JSON data from the `AlbumManager` page handlers. The missing piece of information here is that submission of the HTML form and the handling of its response would be performed by some client-side scripting code via JavaScript that would be able to process the XML or JSON chunk of data accordingly. We will go through this technique in more detail in Chapter 7.

The principles defined above are the basis of what are referred to today as **web services**. A web service is an API provided by a web application so that heterogeneous user agents can interact with the application through formats other than HTML. There are different ways to create web services via REST, SOAP, XML-RPC, Atom, etc. For the purpose of this book we will review REST and the Atom Publishing Protocol as web services for the photoblog application.

REST

Representational State Transfer (REST) is an architecture style for distributed hypermedia systems described by Roy T. Fielding in his dissertation Architectural Styles and the Design of Network-based Software Architectures in 2000.

REST is based on the following elements:

- *Resource*: A resource is the abstract concept of anything. For instance, it can be an image, a blog entry, the current rate between two currencies, a sport result, a mathematical equation, etc.

- *Resource identifier*: Allows components of the distributed system to identify a resource in a unique way.

- *Representation*: A representation of the resource is simply data.

- *Representation metadata*: Information about the representation itself.

- *Resource metadata*: Information about the resource.

- *Control data*: Information about the messages passing through the system between components.

REST also suggests that each message flowing should be **stateless** meaning that it should contain enough information for its processing by the next component within the system and thus should not depend on previous or following messages. Each message is self-contained. This is achieved through the use of resource metadata and representation metadata.

These are the elements describing REST but they are not tied to any underlying protocol. The most commonly used case of REST can be found within the Web and is implemented using the HTTP protocol. In spite of that REST can be implemented using other protocols in other environments.

HTTP is a good candidate to implement REST for the following reasons:

- It is the base of the Web, which is a distributed hypermedia system.

- It is stateless.

- Each request can contain enough information to be processed independently of the rest of the system.

- The content-type and accept headers used by HTTP provide the means to represent a single resource through different representations.

- URIs are powerful and common resource identifiers.

Uniform Resource Identifier

REST is about naming resources on a network and providing a unified mechanism to perform operations on these resources. That's why REST tells us that a resource is identified by at least one identifier. When implementing a REST infrastructure based on the HTTP protocol, these identifiers are defined as **Uniform Resource Identifiers (URIs)**.

Two common subsets of the URI set are:

- **Uniform Resource Locator (URL)**, such as:

  ```
  http://www.cherrypy.org/
  ```

- **Uniform Resource Name (URN)**, such as:

  ```
  urn:isbn:0-201-71088-9
  urn:uuid:13e8cf26-2a25-11db-8693-000ae4ea7d46
  ```

The interesting aspect of URLs is that they contain enough information to locate the resource on the network. Thus in the given URL we know that to locate the resource we need to use the HTTP protocol associated to the HTTP scheme hosted on the host www.cherrypy.org at the path /. (Note, however, that not everyone in the Web community thinks that this multiplexing of capabilities is a positive aspect of URLs but this discussion is out of the scope of this book.)

HTTP Methods

If URIs offer the way to name resources, HTTP methods provide the means by which we can operate on those resources. Let's review the most common methods (also referred to as verbs) in HTTP 1.1.

HTTP Method	Idempotent	Operation
HEAD	Yes	Retrieves the resource metadata. The response is the same as the one to a GET minus the body.
GET	Yes	Retrieves resource metadata and content.
POST	No	Requests the server to create a new resource using the data enclosed in the request body.
PUT	Yes	Requests the server to replace an existing resource with the one enclosed in the request body. The server cannot apply the enclosed resource to a resource not identified by that URI.
DELETE	Yes	Requests the server to remove the resource identified by that URI.
OPTIONS	Yes	Requests the server to return details about capabilities either globally or specifically towards a resource.

The idempotent column of the table indicates whether the request using that particular HTTP method will have the same side-effects with two consecutive identical calls.

By default CherryPy handlers reflect the path of the Request-URI and the handler matches one element of the URI, but as we have seen CherryPy's dispatcher can be changed not to look for the handler within the URI but from the request metadata such as the HTTP method used.

Let's review an example applied to the photoblog application:

```python
import cherrypy
from cherrypy.lib.cptools import accept
from models import Photoblog, Album
from lib.config import conf
from lib.tools import find_acceptable_within

class AlbumRESTService(object):
    exposed = True

    def GET(self, album_id):
        best = accept(['application/xml', 'application/atom+xml',
                       'text/json', 'text/x-json'])



        album = Album.fetch(album_id)
        if not album:
            raise cherrypy.NotFound()

        if best in ['application/xml','application/atom+xml']:
            cherrypy.response.headers['Content-Type'] =
             'application/atom+xml'
            entry = album.to_atom_entry()
            return entry.xml()

        if best in ['application/json', 'text/x-json', 'text/json']:
            cherrypy.response.headers['Content-Type'] =
             'application/json'
            return album.to_json()

        raise cherrypy.HTTPError(400, 'Bad Request')

    def POST(self, title, segment, author, description, content,
             blog_id):
        photoblog = Photoblog.fetch(blog_id)
        if not photoblog:
            raise cherrypy.NotFound()

        album = Album()
```

```
        album.create(photoblog, title, segment, author, description,
                content)
        cherrypy.response.status = '201 Created'
        cherrypy.response.headers['Location'] = '%s/album/%d' %
        (conf.app.base_url, album.ID)

    def PUT(self, album_id, title, segment, author, description,
            content):
        album = Album.fetch(album_id)
        if not album:
            raise cherrypy.NotFound()

        album.update(title, segment, author, description, content)

    def DELETE(self, album_id):
        album = Album.fetch(album_id)
        if album:
            album.delete()
        cherrypy.response.status = '204 No Content'
```

Let's explain what each HTTP method does in this context.

- GET: This returns the representation of the requested resource depending on the `Accept` header. Our application allows `application/xml`, `application/atom+xml`, `text/json`, or `text/x-json`. We use a function called `accept`, which returns the acceptable header found or raises a `cherrypy.HTTPError` (`406, 'Not Acceptable'`) error immediately to inform the user agent that our application cannot deal with its request. Then we verify if the resource still exists; if not, we raise a `cherrypy.NotFound` error, which is a shortcut to `cherrypy.HTTPError(404, 'Not Found')`. Once we have our pre-conditions checked, we return the requested representation of the resource.

  Note that this is equivalent to the `index()` method with the default dispatcher. Bear in mind though that there is no equivalent to the `default()` method when using the method dispatcher.

- POST: The HTTP POST method allows a user agent to create a new resource. The first step is to check if the photoblog that will handle that resource exists. Then we create the resource and we return a status code `201 Created` along with the `Location` header indicating the URI to retrieve the newly created resource.

- PUT: The HTTP PUT method allows the user agent to replace a resource with the one provided in the request body. It is often considered as an update operation. Although RFC 2616 does not forbid PUT to also create a new resource, we will not use it that way in our application as we will explain later.

- DELETE: The DELETE method requests the server to remove the resource. A response to this method can either be 200 OK or 204 No Content. The latter informs the user agent that it should not change its current state since the response has no body.

The (lack of) difference between POST and PUT has long been a source of discussion among web developers. Some consider that having two methods is misleading. Let's try to understand why they are distinct and why we need both.

POST request:

```
POST /album HTTP/1.1
Host: localhost:8080
Content-Length: 77
Content-Type: application/x-www-form-urlencoded

blog_id=1&description=Family&author=sylvain&title=My+family&content=&
segment=
```

POST response:

```
HTTP/1.1 201 Created
Content-Length: 0
Location: http://localhost:8080/album/12
Allow: DELETE, GET, HEAD, POST, PUT
Date: Sun, 21 Jan 2007 16:30:43 GMT
Server: CherryPy/3.0.0
Connection: close
```

PUT request:

```
PUT /album/12 HTTP/1.1
Host: localhost:8080
Content-Length: 69
Content-Type: application/x-www-form-urlencoded

description=Family&author=sylvain&title=Your+family&content=&segment=
```

PUT response:

```
HTTP/1.1 200 OK
Date: Sun, 21 Jan 2007 16:37:12 GMT
Content-Length: 0
Allow: DELETE, GET, HEAD, POST, PUT
Server: CherryPy/3.0.0
Connection: close
```

At first look, two requests seem fairly similar but in fact they have a very important difference, which is the requested URI.

One can POST data to a URI where a process may or may not create a resource whereas in the case of PUT the URI is one of the resources itself and the content sent is the new representation of the resource. In that case, if the resource does not exist yet at that URI, the server can create it if it has been implemented to do so; otherwise the server can return an HTTP error message indicating it is not fulfilling the request. In a nutshell, client POST data to a process but PUT the new representation of the resource identified by the request URI.

One of the root causes of the problem is the fact that many web applications rely only on the POST method to achieve any operation on a resource, whether creating, updating, or deleting it. This is notably the case because these applications often offer only HTML forms, which only support GET and POST, to perform those operations.

Considering the fact that more and more web applications take advantage of separation of concerns and handle submission through client code via JavaScript or external services, it is likely that the use of the PUT and DELETE methods increasing, though it might be a problem in some environments where firewall policies forbid PUT and DELETE requests.

Putting it Together

Our photoblog application will provide a REST interface for the following entities: Album, Film, and Entry. Because of the information they carry, their relationship, and their design we can provide the same interface independent of the entity itself. Therefore we refactor the Album class and create a Resource class that will centralize the implementation of each operation. Each entity-service interface will simply pass the information to the Resource class and let it deal with the hard work. We thus avoid the duplication of code.

```python
import cherrypy
from cherrypy.lib.cptools import accept

from models import Photoblog
from lib import conf
from lib.tools import find_acceptable_within

class Resource(object):

    def handle_GET(self, obj_id):
        best = accept(['application/xml', 'application/atom+xml',
                       'text/json', 'text/x-json',
                       'application/json'])
```

```
        obj = self.__source_class.fetch(obj_id)
        if not obj:
            raise cherrypy.NotFound()

        if best in ['application/xml', 'application/atom+xml']:
            cherrypy.response.headers['Content-Type'] =
                                        'application/atom+xml'
            entry = obj.to_atom_entry()
            return entry.xml()

        if best in ['text/json', 'text/x-json', 'application/json']:
            cherrypy.response.headers['Content-Type'] =
            'application/json'
            return obj.to_json()

        raise cherrypy.HTTPError(400, 'Bad Request')


    def handle_POST(self container_cls, container_id,
                    location_scheme, *args, **kwargs):
        container = container_cls.fetch(container_id)
        if not container:
            raise cherrypy.NotFound()

        obj = self.__source_class()
        obj.create(container, *args, **kwargs)
        cherrypy.response.status = '201 Created'
        cherrypy.response.headers['Location'] = location_scheme %
        (conf.app.base_url, obj.ID)


    def handle_PUT(cls, source_cls, obj_id, *args, **kwargs):
        obj = self.__source_class.fetch(obj_id)
        if not obj:
            raise cherrypy.NotFound()

        obj.update(obj, *args, **kwargs)


    def handle_DELETE(cls, source_cls, obj_id):
        obj = self.__source_class.fetch(obj_id)
        if obj:
            obj.delete(obj)
        cherrypy.response.status = '204 No Content'
```

Then let's redefine our `AlbumRESTService` class to exploit the `Resource` class:

```
from models import Photoblog, Album
from _resource import Resource

class AlbumRESTService(Resource):
    exposed = True
    # The entity class that will be used by the Resource class
    _source_class = Album


    def GET(self, album_id):
        return self.handle_GET(album_id)

    def POST(self, title, segment, author, description, content,
            blog_id):
        self.handle_POST(Photoblog, blog_id, '%s/album/%d',
                        title, segment, author, description,content)

    def PUT(self, album_id, title, segment, author, description,
            content):
        self.handle_PUT(album_id,
                        title, segment, author, description, content)

    def DELETE(self, album_id):
        self.handle_DELETE(album_id)
```

We have now a RESTful interface that will handle the Album resource. Both the Film and Photo entities will be managed the same way. This means that our application will now support requests such as:

```
POST http://somehost.net/service/rest/album/
GET http://somehost.net/service/rest/album/12
PUT http://somehost.net/service/rest/album/12
DELETE http://somehost.net/service/rest/album/12
```

In each of these calls the URI is the unique identifier or name of a resource and the HTTP method is the operation to carry out on that resource.

REST Interface through CherryPy

Until now, we have described services that our photoblog application will support without detailing how to achieve it through CherryPy.

As we have seen in the previous sections HTTP REST relies on HTTP methods to inform a web application of the kind of operation a user agent wishes to carry out. In order to implement REST through CherryPy for our photoblog application we will use the HTTP method dispatcher as reviewed in Chapter 4 to handle incoming requests to the service classes defined above, something along these lines:

```
rest_service = Service()
rest_service.album = AlbumRESTService()
conf = {'/': {'request.dispatch': cherrypy.dispatch.
MethodDispatcher()}}
cherrypy.tree.mount(rest_service, '/service/rest', config=conf)
```

This implies that requests applying to a URI path such as `/service/rest/album/` will be applied in a REST spirit.

REST is quite a common term but building true RESTful applications can be a difficult task. The difficulty resides in defining a sensible and meaningful URI set associated with the application resources. In other words, the difficult part lies in the designing of the API. This section should have introduced you to the principles behind REST but developing the architecture of a large system around REST requires a high-level understanding of the resources dealt with, their naming convention, and their relationship.

Atom Publishing Protocol

In the previous section we have introduced REST and showed how it can be used as a service for web applications. In this section we will introduce the **Atom Publishing Protocol (APP)**, which at the time of writing this book was on its way to becoming a new IETF standard. This means that some aspects of this section might no longer be up to date by the time you read them.

APP has arisen from the Atom community as an application-level protocol on top of HTTP to allow the publishing and editing of web resources. The unit of messages between an APP server and a client is based on the Atom XML-document format defined in RFC 4287.

Although APP is not specified as being an implementation of the REST principles, the protocol does follow the same ideas, which give it a RESTful aspect. Therefore, many of the principles of the previous section will apply here; but first let's overview the Atom XML-document format.

Atom XML-Document Format

The Atom XML-document format describes a set of information through two top-level elements:

- Feed: A feed consists of:
    - ○ metadata (sometimes referred as the *head* of the feed)
    - ○ zero or more entries

- Entry: An entry is made up of:
    - ○ metadata
    - ○ some content

Example of an Atom 1.0 feed document as per RFC4287:

```
<?xml version="1.0" encoding="utf-8"?>
<feed xmlns="http://www.w3.org/2005/Atom">
  <title>Photoblog feed</title>
  <published>2006-08-13T10:57:18Z</published>
  <updated>2006-08-13T11:18:01Z</updated>
  <link rel="self" href="http://host/blog/feed/album/"
                                  type="application/atom+xml" />
  <author>
    <name>Sylvain Hellegouarch</name>
  </author>
  <id>urn:uuid:13e8cf26-2a25-11db-8693-000ae4ea7d46</id>
  <entry>
    <title>This is my family album</title>
    <id>urn:uuid:25cd2014-2ab3-11db-902d-000ae4ea7d46</id>
    <link rel="self" href="http://host/blog/feed/album/12"
      type="application/atom+xml" />
    <link rel="alternate" href="http://host/blog/album/12"
      type="text/html" />
    <updated>2006-08-13T11:18:01Z</updated>
    <content type="text">Some content</content>
  </entry>
</feed>
```

A web application can serve Atom documents for subscription thus providing a way for user agents to syndicate themselves to information the application developer chooses to provide.

Our photoblog application will provide Atom feeds of the following entities:

- Photoblog: Each entry of the feed will link to an album feed of the blog.
- Album: Each entry of the feed will link to a film feed of the album.
- Film: Each entry will relate to a photo of the film.

We will not explain every element of an Atom document but review a few of the most common ones.

- id, title, and updated are compulsory elements in any feed or entry.
    - id must be an IRI as defined in RFC 3987 as a complement to URIs
    - updated must follow RFC 3339. RFC 4287 says that this element only needs to be updated when the modification is semantically significant.
- author is compulsory within an Atom feed whether in the feed element, entry element, or both. However, entries of a feed can inherit the feed author element if they do not provide one.
- link is not mandatory but is recommended and very useful to provide the following:
    - the URI of the resource associated to the entry or the feed using rel="self"
    - the URI of alternative representations of the resource using rel="alternate" and specifying the media-type of the resource
    - the URI to related resources using rel="related"
- content should be present at most once. Either the content of an entry is inlined within the entry as text, escaped HTML or XHTML, or the content is referenced by the src attribute providing the URI of the actual content.

Thus we will have for a film feed:

```xml
<?xml version="1.0" encoding="UTF-8"?>
<feed xmlns="http://www.w3.org/2005/Atom">
    <id>urn:uuid:8ed4ae87-2ac9-11db-b2c4-000ae4ea7d46</id>
    <title>Film of my holiday</title>
    <updated>2006-08-13T13:50:49Z</updated>
    <author>
        <name>Sylvain Hellegouarch</name>
    </author>
    <entry>
        <id>urn:uuid:41548439-c12d-48b5-baec-a72b1bf8576f</id>
        <published>2006-08-13T13:45:38Z</published>
        <updated>2006-08-13T13:50:49Z</updated>
        <title>At the beach</title>
        <link rel="self" href="http://host/feed/photo/at-the-beach"
         type="application/atom+xml"/>
        <link rel="alternate" href="http://host/photo/at-the-beach"
         type="text/html" />
```

```
            <content src="http://host/media/IMAGE001.png"
              type="image/png" />
        </entry>
    </feed>
```

The Atom format is commonly used in the blog environment to allow users to subscribe to it. However, thanks to its flexibility and extensibility the Atom format is now used in different contexts such as publishing, archiving, and exporting content.

APP Implementation

The aim of providing an **Atom Publishing Protocol (APP)** implementation within the photoblog application is to introduce the protocol and to provide two different services demonstrating the benefits of the separation of concerns. Because APP is not yet a standard and because at the time of writing this book it was under a fairly good amount of discussion, it is possible that by the time you read this section our implementation will no longer be compliant. However, there is minimum risk as the current version of the protocol draft, i.e. 13, seems stable enough regarding its main characteristics.

The Atom Publishing Protocol defines a set of operations between an APP service and a user-agent using HTTP and its mechanisms and the Atom XML-document format as the unit of messages.

APP first defines a service document, which provides the user agent with the URI of the different collections served by the APP service. It is of the form:

```
<?xml version="1.0" encoding="UTF-8"?>
<service xmlns="http://purl.org/atom/app#" xmlns:atom=
  "http://www.w3.org/2005/Atom">
  <workspace>
    <collection href="http://host/service/atompub/album/">
      <atom:title>Friends Albums</atom:title>
    <categories fixed="yes">
        <atom:category term="friends" />
      </categories>
    </collection>
    <collection href="http://host/service/atompub/film/">
      <atom:title>Films</atom:title>
      <accept>image/png, image/jpeg</accept>
    </collection>
  </workspace>
</service>
```

Once a user agent has fetched that service document it knows there are two collections available. The first collection informs the user-agent that it will only accept Atom documents that have a category matching the one defined. The second collection will only accept data with the image/png or image/jpeg MIME types.

Collections are the containers of what APP refers to as members. The operation of creating a member is done against a collection but operations of retrieving, updating, and deleting are done against that member itself and not the collection.

A collection is represented as an Atom feed in which entries are referred as to members. The critical addition to the Atom entry is the use of an Atom link with the rel attribute set to edit to describe the member resource. By setting this attribute to this value we indicate that the href attribute of the link element references the URL of the member resource that can be retrieved, edited, and deleted at that URI. An Atom entry containing such a link element is called a **member** of a collection.

APP specifies how to perform the basic CRUD operations against a member of a collection or the collection itself by using HTTP methods as described in the following table.

Operation	HTTP Method	Status Code	Returned Content
Retrieve	GET	200	An Atom entry representing the resource
Create	POST	201	An Atom entry representing the resource
			The URI of the newly created resource via the Location and Content-Location headers
Update	PUT	200	An Atom entry representing the resource
Delete	DELETE	200	None

When creating or updating a resource, the APP server is free to modify part of the resource such as its id, its updated value, etc. Therefore user agents should not rely on their version of the resource and always synchronize with the server.

Although members of a collection are Atom entries, it is not compulsory to create a new member by submitting an Atom entry. APP supports any media type as long as it is allowed through the app:accept element of an app:collection element. That element takes a comma-separated list of media types specifying to the client which content types the collection will process on POST requests.

If you POST a PNG image to a collection that accepts it, the server will create at least two resources.

- A member resource, which can be seen as the metadata of the image
- A media resource

Remember that an APP server has total control over the content sent and therefore it is imaginable that an APP server could convert the PNG content to JPEG before storing it. A client cannot assume that the content or resource sent will be copied, as done by a server. In any case the server returns the member resource when creation has succeeded (please refer to the APP specification for detailed examples) and this is precisely what makes APP so powerful, since whichever type of resource a server says it handles APP ensures that metadata will be generated under the form of an Atom entry.

In addition to defining an interface to manipulate members within a collection, APP provides support for paging when a collection gets too big. This allows the user agent to request a given range of members within a collection. We will not explain this feature but you can review the APP specification if you are interested in this feature.

Furthermore, since the photoblog application will follow the REST principles as closely as possible for implementing APP, we invite you to refer yourself to the REST section for more specific details on how APP uses REST principles.

In this section, we have briefly presented the Atom Publishing Protocol, a protocol based on the Atom XML-document format to allow the publishing of heterogeneous data types. In spite of not yet being an official standard, APP already interests many organizations and it is quite likely you will find it in more and more applications.

Summary

This chapter has introduced you to the concept of web services, which defines the idea of offering an API via common web protocols such as HTTP. By providing such APIs your web application becomes much more flexible, powerful, and extensible. Web services are not a must-have feature though and not every web application would offer them. Our photoblog application, in its spirit of demonstrating some of the common modern web techniques, uses them as an example rather than as a compulsory feature. However, by reviewing the code of our photoblog application you will understand some of the interesting benefits of web services, which will hopefully give you ideas for your own applications.

7
The Presentation Layer

Until now, we have developed our application from a server-side point of view. In this chapter, we will start focusing on the client side of the photoblog. Initially, we will introduce HTML templating via the `Kid` Python engine and JavaScript via the Mochikit library. We will present briefly a few important components of the success of the Web such as HTML, XHTML, and CSS. However, these sections do not aim at explaining each of them deeply, as this is out of the scope of this book.

HTML

Although in our previous chapter, we introduced the separation of concerns between layers within our application, we need to keep in mind that our primary target is Internet browsers, so we will focus on HTML rendering.

HTML (HyperText Markup Language), used right from the beginning of the Web as defined by Tim Berners-Lee in the early 1990s, is a light version of **SGML (Standard Generalized Markup Language)** keeping only simple elements that are useful for the Web. Due to the quick growth of the Web, further development was achieved on HTML to improve it. Eventually HTML 4.0 was officially specified in 1997 by the W3C with an update in 1999 leading to HTML 4.01, which is still as of today the official version to use.

Example of an HTML 4.01 document:

```
<!DOCTYPE html PUBLIC "-//W3C//DTD HTML 4.01//EN" "http://www.w3.org/
TR/html4/strict.dtd">
<html>
  <head>
    <title>Hello World!</title>
  </head>
  <body>
```

```
    <p>Not much to say really.</p>
  </body>
</html>
```

The first line of the document states the DOCTYPE declaration, specifying which variant of a format a document follows. DOCTYPEs are specified in DTDs (Document Type Definitions).

XML

In 1996, W3C started to work on **XML (Extensible Markup Language)**, a generic simpler markup language derived from SGML keeping its power while avoiding its complexity. In the context of the Web, the goal of XML is aimed at solving a few limitations of HTML, such as the lack of:

- **Extensibility**: HTML did not allow new elements to be added to the language.

- **Validation**: HTML did not offer a language to validate against the structure nor the semantics of a document.

- **Structure**: HTML did not allow complex structures.

XHTML

Due to XML, expressive and flexible work was undertaken by W3C to reformulate HTML 4 through XML, leading to specification of XHTML 1.0 in the year 2000.

XHTML 1.0 has the following features:

- User agents that solely understand HTML 4 can render a document, making it backward compatible.

- Publishers can enter the XML world and its richness.

Example of an XHTML 1.0 document:

```
<?xml version="1.0" encoding="utf-8"?>
<!DOCTYPE html PUBLIC "-//W3C//DTD XHTML 1.0 Strict//EN"
    "http://www.w3.org/TR/xhtml1/DTD/xhtml1-strict.dtd">
<html xmlns="http://www.w3.org/1999/xhtml">
  <head>
    <title>Hello World!</title>
  </head>
  <body>
```

```
    <p>Not much to say really.</p>
  </body>
</html>
```

In this example, we also specify a DOCTYPE declaration informing consumers that our document respects the XHTML 1.0 Strict DTD. Since XHTML is an application of XML:

- We provide the XML declaration on the very first line to give the XML-consuming processor some hints about the document content, such as the fact that it is encoded in UTF-8. Note that it is not compulsory.

- We also explicitly mark the anonymous namespace of that document as the XHTML namespace.

Although the syntax for both the documents is very close, they carry different semantics and would be treated differently by user agents. Therefore, both the documents have distinct MIME formats. An HTML document should be served using the `text/html` MIME content-type, while XHTML documents should be served via `application/xhtml+xml`. However, because XHTML 1.0 aims at being backward compatible with user agents that do not understand its MIME content-type, it is allowed to serve an XHTML 1.0 document respecting specific guidelines as `text/html`. This is, however, not recommended and can lead to unexpected rendering that depends on how user agents treat the structure of the document; it is often referred as *tag-soup*.

For these reasons, serving XHTML can be cumbersome on the Internet and is the root of extremely heated discussions. Our photoblog application will therefore keep it simple by using HTML.

CSS

Whether you use HTML or XHTML, both formats only specify the structure and the semantics of your pages; they do not inform user agents how they ought to render those pages. This is achieved through CSS (Cascading Style Sheets), a language to describe rules to apply on elements within a marked up document such as HTML or XHTML. A rule is structured as follows:

- A *selector* indicates the element on which the rule is to be applied. The selector can be precise to target only one specific element within the context of the document or applicable to all.

- One or more *attributes* indicate which property of the element is involved.

- A *value* or a set of values is associated to each attribute.

An example applied to the previous HTML example is as follows:

```
<!DOCTYPE html PUBLIC "-//W3C//DTD HTML 4.01//EN" "http://www.w3.org/
TR/html4/strict.dtd">
<html>
  <head>
    <title>Hello World!</title>
    <style type="text/css">
    body
    {
      background-color: #666633;
      color: #fff;
    }

    p
    {
      text-align: center;
    }
    </style>
  </head>
  <body>
    <p>Not much to say really.</p>
  </body>
</html>
```

In this example:

- body is the selector.
- background-color is the attribute, whose value is #666633.

In the previous example, we have embedded the CSS within the HTML document itself. It is advisable to externalize it into its own document and link it from the HTML page, as follows:

```
<!DOCTYPE html PUBLIC "-//W3C//DTD HTML 4.01//EN"
        "http://www.w3.org/TR/html4/strict.dtd">
<html>
  <head>
    <title>Hello World!</title>
    <link rel="stylesheet" href="style.css">
  </head>
  <body>
    <p>Not much to say really.</p>
  </body>
</html>
```

The CSS file, `style.css`, is as follows:

```
body
{
  background-color: #663;
  color: #fff;
}
p
{
  text-align: center;
}
```

DHTML

When Tim Berners-Lee imagined the Web, he did so to enable the exchange of documents between researchers. Those documents were static and were not generated by the web application. In fact, web applications did not exist at that time, only web servers that were accepting requests and returning content. Since then, the Web has grown much more value and web applications are a reality. Nonetheless, for a long time the component achieving the work has been the server itself, the client only being required to display the rendered content. Quickly enough however, it appeared that providing much fancier interfaces would move the Web one step further for it to attract a larger public. The Web should, could, and would be more than presenting books or papers on a screen.

The term DHTML (Dynamic HTML) was coined to group a set of technologies to improve client-side content handling. DHTML encompasses:

- HTML defining the structure of the document to manipulate
- CSS to style the web page
- JavaScript to dynamically modify the Document Object Model (DOM)

A DOM is a memory representation of the (X)HTML document structure built by the browser. By using JavaScript functions, it is possible to dynamically modify the DOM tree and thus change its rendering from the end-user perspective.

However interesting the idea behind DHTML was, it never really took off due to interoperability issues between browser vendors. JavaScript and CSS were not implemented equally across navigators making it really hard for web developers to ensure their page would act as expected in most cases. Nowadays, DHTML is not a common term in the field but its ideas have been kept and improved in newer techniques. This has been also possible thanks to a better interoperability between browsers, better debugging tools, and the arrival of dedicated JavaScript toolkits or frameworks encapsulating browser differences in a common API, as we will see later on.

Templating

In the previous sections, we have introduced the basic components that constitute web pages—HTML or XHTML for the structure and CSS for the style. Generating web pages can be as easy as using your favorite text editor and laying it down. However in the context of a dynamic application, where the content is based on a given context and generated on the fly, you need tools to ease such creation. This is achieved through the use of templating engines. A templating engine takes a model of the page as well as the input data and then processes both to render the final page.

When searching for a templating engine, you should look for one that offers at least some features such as:

- Variable substitution: In your template, a variable can act as place holder for your input.

- Conditional statements: It is common that a template needs to be rendered with slight differences based on the context of the input data.

- Looping mechanism: This is obviously mandatory when your template has to render a set of data into a table for example.

- Extensibility: Templates can often share aspects and diverge in some specific contexts, for example common header and footer templates.

The Python world is anything but short in templating engines, and selecting one for your needs will certainly be a matter of taste based on its features as well as its syntax. For the purpose of this book, we will use a templating engine named Kid developed by Ryan Tomayko.

Kid—The Templating Engine

Now, we will have some description of our Kid engine.

Overview

Let's start our introduction to the Kid engine by creating a template of our previous examples:

```
<!DOCTYPE html PUBLIC "-//W3C//DTD HTML 4.01//EN" "http://www.w3.org/
TR/html4/strict.dtd">
<html xmlns:py="http://purl.org/kid/ns#">
  <head>
    <title>${title}</title>
    <link rel="stylesheet" href="style.css" />
  </head>
```

```
  <body>
    <p>${message}</p>
  </body>
</html>
```

As you can see, a template looks very similar to the final expected rendered page. When you save this template in a file named `helloworld.kid`, the next step is to process the template via the `Kid` engine as follows:

```
import kid
params = {'title': 'Hello world', 'message': 'Not much to say.'}
t = kid.Template('helloworld.kid', **params)
print t.serialize(output='html')
```

`Kid` provides a `Template` function that requires the name of the template to be processed and the input data to be passed on during the rendering of the template. When a template is being processed for the first time, `Kid` creates a Python module that serves as a cached version of the template for latter use. The `kid.Template` function returns an instance of the `Template` class you then use to render the output content. To do so, the `Template` class provides the following methods:

- `serialize`: This returns the output content as a Python string.
- `generate`: This returns the output content as a Python iterator.
- `write`: This dumps the output content into a file object.

These three methods take the following parameters:

- `encoding`: This informs `Kid` how to encode the output content; it defaults to UTF-8.
- `fragment`: This is a Boolean value asking `Kid` to include or not the XML prolog or Doctype in the final result.
- `output`: This specifies which type of serialization should be used by `Kid` to render the content.

Kid's Attributes

The attributes of Kid are as follows:

XML-Based Templating Language

Kid is an XML-based language, which means:

- A Kid template must be a well-formed XML document.

- Kid uses attributes within XML elements to inform the underlying engine what action to follow when reaching an element. To avoid collision with other existing attributes within the XML document, Kid comes with its own namespace (http://purl.org/kid/ns#), most of the time associated with the py prefix, for example:

  ```
  <p py:if="...">...</p>
  ```

Variable Substitution

Kid comes with a very simple variable substitution scheme: ${variable-name}.

This can be used either in attributes of elements or as the text content of an element. Kid will evaluate the variable each time it comes across it in the template.

If you need to output a literal string such as ${something}, you can escape the variable substitution by doubling the dollar sign such as $${something}, which will be rendered as ${something}.

Conditional Statement

When you need to toggle between different cases in a template, you need to use the following syntax:

```
<tag py:if="expression">...</tag>
```

Where:

- tag is the name of the element, for instance DIV or SPAN.

- expression is a Python expression. If as a Boolean it evaluates to True the element will be included in the output content. Otherwise, the element will not be part of it.

Looping Mechanism

To tell `Kid` to loop on an element, you must use the following syntax:

```
<tag py:for="expression">...</tag>
```

Where:

- `tag` is the name of the element.
- `expression` is a Python expression, for example `for value in [...]`.

The looping mechanism is as follows:

```
<!DOCTYPE html PUBLIC "-//W3C//DTD HTML 4.01//EN" "http://www.w3.org/
TR/html4/strict.dtd">
<html xmlns:py="http://purl.org/kid/ns#">
  <head>
    <title>${title}</title>
    <link rel="stylesheet" href="style.css" />
  </head>
  <body>
    <table>
      <caption>A few songs</caption>
      <tr>
        <th>Artist</th>
        <th>Album</th>
        <th>Title</th>
      </tr>
      <tr py:for="info in infos">
        <td>${info['artist']}</td>
        <td>${info['album']}</td>
        <td>${info['song']}</td>
      </tr>
    </table>
  </body>
</html>


import kid

# Fake object and method which suggests that we pull the data to be
# rendered from a database in the form of a Python dictionary.

params = discography.retrieve_songs()

t = kid.Template('songs.kid', **params)
print t.serialize(output='html')
```

Extensibility

Extending a template is done using the following syntax:

```
<tag py:extends="templates">...</tag>
```

Where:

- `tag` is the name of the element. In this specific case however, the element can only be the root element of the current template.

- `templates` is a comma-separated list of `Kid` template filenames or instances.

First, define a `Kid` template named `common.kid`:

```
<html xmlns:py="http://purl.org/kid/ns#">
  <head py:match="item.tag == 'this-is-ed'">
    <title>${title}</title>
    <link rel="stylesheet" href="style.css" />
  </head>
</html>
```

Then, modify the template of the previous example:

```
<!DOCTYPE html PUBLIC "-//W3C//DTD HTML 4.01//EN" "http://www.w3.org/
TR/html4/strict.dtd">
<html py:extends="'common.kid'" xmlns:py="http://purl.org/kid/ns#">
...
...
  <body>
    <table>
    <caption>A few songs</caption>
    <tr>
    <th>Artist</th>
    <th>Album</th>
    <th>Title</th>
    </tr>
    <tr py:for="info in infos">
    <td>${info['artist']}</td>
    <td>${info['album']}</td>
    <td>${info['song']}</td>
    </tr>
    </table>
  </body>
</html>
```

When `Kid` processes that template, it will first compile the `common.kid` template. When `Kid` meets the `<this-is-ed />` element, it will understand that it matches the head element of the `common.kid` template, and will replace its content.

Other Attributes

Kid comes with more attributes to the basic ones we have reviewed before:

- py:content="expression": The descendant of the element using this attribute will be replaced by the output content of the expression.

- py:strip="expression": If the expression evaluates to True, the containing element will not be present in the result but its descendants will be there. If the expression evaluates to False, the processing goes as normal.

- py:replace="expression": This is a shortcut for py:content="expression" py:strip="True".

- py:attrs="expression": This allows dynamic insertion of new attributes into the element.

- py:def="template_name(args)": This allows creation of a temporary template that can be referenced elsewhere in the main template.

You can get more information by navigating to the official Kid documentation available at http://kid-templating.org/.

Photoblog Design Preparation

In the previous sections, we have introduced tools that we will use to create our application interface. In the following sections, we will create the base of that interface.

Targetting the User Agent

Considering the fact that the photoblog application is centered on the images to be displayed, we will disregard user agents not supporting that feature. The application will also heavily use client-side code through JavaScript. Thus, we will solely focus on the modern browser engines supporting it.

Here is a brief list of our principal targets:

Engine	Browsers Targeted
Gecko	Mozilla Firefox 1.5 and above, Netscape 8
MSHTML	Internet Explorer 6 SP1 and above
KHTML (and WebKit)	Konqueror, Safari
Presto	Opera 9 and above

Tools

For this application you will need:

- A text editor; your favorite text editor will do.
- A browser providing development tools; Mozilla Firefox with the following extensions would be a good choice:
  - Web developer or Firebug
  - LiveHTTPHeader or Tamper Data. Alternatively, CherryPy provides the `log_headers` tool, which when enabled in the global settings of CherryPy will log the request headers on the server allowing an easy debugging per request.
  - DOM inspector
  - JavaScript debugger

Moreover, although we will be doing most of our development using one specific browser, it is recommended to test it regularly using as many browsers as you can.

Global Design Goals

As we said, the photoblog application is focused on images. With this in mind, we will draw a globally designed interface, as follows:

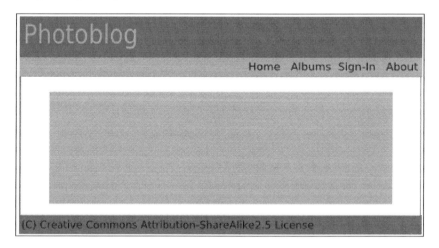

As you can see, our default design will not have the fanciest look but it provides us with the basic structure for a blog that we are looking for, to explore web design.

The topmost area will be our header. This is where you will put the catchy name of your blog. Right under it we will have the navigation menu with a few links to move through the base areas of the blog. Then we will have the content area where we will only display by default photography. It means that by default no text will be displayed and it will require user interaction to reveal it. This ensures that the focus stays on the photography. However, the content area will stretch as requested, when it has to display text content. Finally, there is a footer area containing information about the copyrights of the content of this blog.

Design Directory Layout

The design that we will use for the photoblog application will reside in the following directory structure:

```
default\
  commond.kid
  index.kid
  css\
    style.css
  images\
  js\
```

We will name this design *default*, as it will be the one shipped with the application and used by default during the first access to the application.

You will note that the `js` directory is empty in spite of intensive use of JavaScript. The reason is that we will define a global static directory of files that might be shared by different templates, which could be the case with all the JavaScript files we will create.

CherryPy—Encapsulating the Template Rendering Process

CherryPy handlers could well be fine calling `Kid` themselves and returning the serialized output of a template but we will not do it that way. Instead, we will encapsulate `Kid` into a CherryPy tool that our handlers will call. There are two reasons for such a decision:

- To allow you to switch from `Kid` to a different templating engine. Imagine that you prefer the `Cheetah` templating engine to `Kid`. You could write a template with `Cheetah` and only modify the tool without having to go through the entire application.

- To ease the maintenance. If `Kid` evolves and changes its syntax, it will be easier to update just the tool rather than the entire application.

The tool named `Design` is attached to the default CherryPy toolbox:

```
import os.path

import cherrypy
from cherrypy import Tool, tools
import kid

def transform(path=None, template=None):
    params = cherrypy.response.body
    if path and template and isinstance(params, dict):
        path = os.path.normpath(os.path.join(path, template + '.kid'))

        template = kid.Template(file=path, **params)
        cherrypy.response.body = template.generate(output='html')

# Attach our Design tool to the CherryPy default toolbox
tools.design = Tool("before_finalize", transform)
```

Then we will use the tool like this:

```
@cherrypy.expose
@cherrypy.tools.design(template='index')
def index(self):
    return {...}
```

A page handler using that tool will be required to return a Python dictionary containing values to be passed to the templating engine and expected by the template.

Note also that the tool expects a `path` parameter that will not be passed to the decorator call itself. That `path` represents the absolute base path of the folder containing a design directory and in our example `path` would be the `default` directory that we have already defined. We will set this value once in a configuration file that will be attached to the CherryPy application. We will see more details about this in Chapter 10.

Christian Wyglendowski is the maintainer of a project called Buffet that aims at providing the core feature demonstrated in the mentioned tool. It supports many templating languages and offers an extended API. However, it currently supports solely CherryPy 2 and therefore it is not used in this chapter. CherryPy 3 support is planned and will certainly be available soon.

Photoblog Design in Detail

Now, we will have a look at the basic structure of our photoblog design.

Basic Structure

Our first step is to define the HTML structure of the page:

```
<!DOCTYPE HTML PUBLIC "-//W3C//DTD HTML 4.01//EN"
          "http://www.w3.org/TR/html4/strict.dtd">
<html py:extends="'common.kid'" xmlns:py="http://purl.org/kid/ns#">
  <head />
  <body>
    <!-- main container of our content -->
    <div id="page">
      <div id="header">
        <br />
      </div>
      <div id="nav">
        <ul>
          <li><a href="/">Home</a></li>
          <li><a href="/">Albums</a></li>
          <li><a href="/">Sign-In</a></li>
          <li><a href="/">About</a></li>
        </ul>
      </div>
      <!-- content area where we will display the picture
                   and other content such as forms -->
      <div id="content-pane">
        <div id="photo-pane">
          <img id="photo-data" src="" alt="" /><br />
        </div>
      </div>
      <div id="footer">
        <br />
      </div>
    </div>
  </body>
</html>
```

This template, which we will name `index.kid`, extends the template `common.kid`. It looks as follows:

```
<html xmlns:py="http://purl.org/kid/ns#">
  <head py:match="item.tag == 'head'">
    <title></title>
    <meta http-equiv="content-type" content="text/html;
                        charset=iso-8859-1"> </meta>
  </head>
</html>
```

The `head` element of the `index.kid` template will be replaced by that of the `Kid` template named `common.kid`.

We will process that template as follows:

```
import cherrypy
import kid

class Root:
  @cherrypy.expose
  def index(self):
    t = kid.Template('index.kid')
    return t.generate(output='html')

if __name__ == '__main__':
  import os.path
  cur_dir = os.getcwd()
  conf = {'/style.css': {'tools.staticfile.on': \
          True,'tools.staticfile.filename': os.path.join(cur_dir, \
                                          'style.css')}}
  cherrypy.quickstart(Root(), config=conf)
```

Now if you navigate to `http://localhost:8080/`, it should look as follows:

The next step is to add the CSS stylesheet by modifying the `common.kid` template:

```
<html xmlns:py="http://purl.org/kid/ns#">
  <head py:match="item.tag == 'head'">
    <title></title>
    <meta http-equiv="content-type" content="text/html;
                                  charset=iso-8859-1">
    </meta>
    <link rel="stylesheet" type="text/css" href="/style.css"> </link>
  </head>
</html>
```

Then, we define the CSS as follows:

```
body
{
  background-color: #ffffff;
  font-family: sans-serif;
  font-size: small;
  line-height: 1.3em;
  text-align: center;
}

#page
{
  position:relative;
  top: 25px;
  margin: 0px auto;
  text-align:left;
  width: 600px;
  position: left;
  border: 1px #ffffff solid;
  }

#header
{
  height: 45px;
  background-color: #71896D;
  border-bottom: 2px #858A6E solid;
}

#nav
{
  height: 20px;
  background-color: #CED6AB;
```

```
    border-bottom: 2px #858A6E solid;
    font-weight: bold;
    text-align: right;
}

#nav ul
{
    margin: 0 0 0 20px;
    padding: 0;
    list-style-type: none;
}

#nav li
{
    display: inline;
    padding: 0 10px;
}

#nav li a
{
    text-decoration: none;
    color: #858A6E;
}

#nav li a:hover
{
    text-decoration: none;
    color: #999966;
}

#content-pane
{
    background-color: #ffffff;
    border-bottom: 1px #858A6E solid;
    text-align: center;
    padding: 50px 50px 50px 50px;
}

#photo-pane img
{
    border: 1px #858A6E solid;
    padding: 3px 3px 3px 3px;
}
```

```
#footer
{
  height: 20px;
  background-color: #CED6AB;
}
```

Now, if you reload the page, you should see something like this:

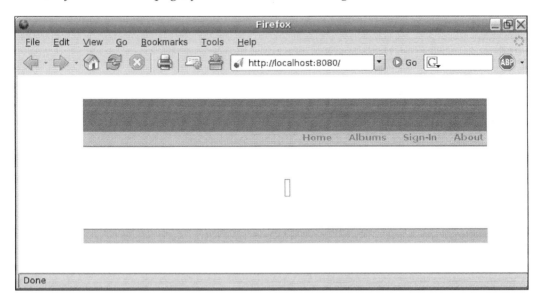

We now have the main page of our photoblog application. The following configurations will make us understand how we will handle the other pages of our application:

- One Kid template per page: In this configuration, each time a link is followed or a form is submitted to the application, a new page will be constructed on the server from its template and will be sent back to the browser.
  - ○ Advantage: It is easy for the web designer who can now edit every page.
  - ○ Drawback: It feels less dynamic from the end-user point of view. It feels as if the navigation is done *per page*.

- One or two templates and a bunch of JavaScript files: In this case, only one page would be sent to the browser but it will contain enough information for the browser to generate and insert blocks of content depending on the context and end-user interaction.

  - Advantage: It feels much more dynamic for the end-user. Less processing is done by the server, which sends data to be processed by the user agent.

  - Drawback: It is less intuitive for the web designer. It will not work on user agents that do not support JavaScript.

- One Kid template per block of content to be displayed: This is a mix between the previous two solutions. One page will be sent to the user agent and upon user interaction, the browser will go and fetch extra blocks of content generated on the server from the Kid templates that will be inserted directly within the web page. This technique is referred as AHAH (Asynchronous HTML and HTTP), as we will see in the next chapter.

  - Advantage: It is easy for the web developer who works on HTML code, as in the first solution.

  - Drawback: The rendering is done by the server, so more work on its part. It does not work for browsers that do not support JavaScript.

For the purpose of this application, we will be using mainly the second solution. We will see the application in the upcoming sections.

Mochikit

Mochikit, created and maintained by Bob Ippolito, is a JavaScript toolkit providing a set of functionalities to simplify the development of web applications from a client-side perspective. Mochikit provides the following components:

- **Async**: This allows HTTP requests from the browser that are handled either synchronously or asynchronously. We will explain this in more detail in the next chapter.

- **Base**: This is a set of functions for common programming tasks.

- **DOM**: This is an API to ease the manipulation of the DOM tree and perform operations such as insertion or removal of nodes in the tree.

- **DragAndDrop**: This is there to enable drag and drop handling in a web application.

- **Color**: This provides color abstraction with support for CSS3 colors that are not supported natively by current browsers.

- **DateTime**: These are helpers for date and time management.

- **Format**: These are helpers for string manipulation.

- **Iter**: This brings good support to JavaScript for the iterator pattern over a collection of data.

- **Logging** and **LoggingPane**: These are extended logger tools.

- **Signal**: This is an API to handle events and their dispatching in a web application.

- **Style**: This is a better support for CSS.

- **Sortable**: This simplifies the way to sort collections of data.

- **Visual**: These are effects to make a web application more attractive.

Mochikit is not the only major player in the JavaScript toolkit field; there are others such Dojo, script.aculo.us, Rico, Yahoo UI Library, JQuery, mooh.fx, etc. All of them allow you to write rich client-side web applications and choosing one of these is a matter of taste as much as of functionalities.

We will use the Mochikit library extensively to provide a more dynamic feeling experience to the end user.

For example, we could add a box displaying information about the film associated to the current photograph displayed. This box would be hidden by default and would show up when the user clicks on a link.

Developing the Photoblog Design

We have now all the tools to develop a web application interface and we will now present step by step how our photoblog application will use those tools through specific examples, reflecting the application user-interface cases.

HTML Code

Let's start first by the insertion of an HTML box that will display film information.

The HTML code of the box to be inserted into the `index.kid` template:

```
<div id="film-pane">
  <div id="film-infos-pane">
    <label class="infos-label">Title:</label>
    <span class="infos-content">My last holiday</span>
```

```
    <label class="infos-label">Created on:</label>
    <span class="infos-content">18th August, 2006</span>
    <label class="infos-label">Updated on:</label>
    <span class="infos-content">27th August, 2006</span>
    <label class="infos-label">Description:</label>
    <span class="infos-content">Some text here...</span>
  </div>
</div>
```

As you can see, we define an inner box and an outer box because we may need to add more content sharing the same process as the inner box. Note also that we do provide some random data from the template itself for testing purpose while developing the interface. Indeed, even though the application is built step by step in this book, in real-life projects tasks are usually achieved in parallel, so the areas that are normally interdependent have to work on their side on mock-up objects or data. Those are hard-coded but provide realistic content to work against.

Adding a Link

As this box will be hidden by default, we need to provide the end user with a link to toggle its visibility. To do so, we add the following HTML code to the `index.kid` template:

```
<span id="toggle-film-infos">Film information</span>
```

Note that, although we call it a link, this is not an HTML <a /> element but instead a text label that will act as a link from the end-user point of view.

Handling the End-User Actions

Assuming we have a JavaScript file named `utils.js`, we would define:

```
function toggleFilmVisibility(e)
{
  toggle($('film-pane'), 'slide');
}

function initialize(e)
{
  hideElement($('film-pane'));
  connect('toggle-film-infos', 'onclick', toggleFilmVisibility);
};


connect(window, 'onload', initialize);
```

First, we create a simple JavaScript function that takes only one parameter, a DOM event object containing details of the current event, the caller, and the callee. This function performs solely two actions:

- It hides the DOM element with `film-pane` as `id`. Mochikit provides the `$(name)` as a shortcut to retrieve a DOM node within the DOM tree.

- It attaches the `onclick` signal of the element with the `id` named `toggle-film-infos` to a function named `toggleFilmVisibility`. That function only toggles the state of visibility of the film box.

Then, we connect the `onload` signal of the `window` DOM object with the `initialize` function. This means that `initialize` will be called once the `window` object has been loaded.

Amending the Template

In the `common.kid` template, we simply need to add the following lines to the `<head />` element:

```
<script type="application/javascript" src="/MochiKit/MochiKit.js" />
<script type="application/javascript" src="/MochiKit/New.js" />
<script type="application/javascript" src="/utils.js" />
```

Amending the CSS

As we have seen in our example, our different HTML elements have either an `id` attribute and/or a `class` attribute. Both will allow us to apply a specific style to those elements, as we will see now:

```
/* will inform the end-user the text is clickable as link */
span#toggle-film-infos
{
  cursor: pointer;
  text-align: left;
}

span#toggle-film-infos:hover
{
  text-decoration: underline;
}

#film-pane
{
  border: 1px #663 solid;
```

```
      padding: 3px 3px 3px 3px;
      background-color: #fff;
}
#film-infos-pane
{
   text-align: left;
}


/* the following rules allow the information to be
               organized and displayed as in table */
infos-content, .infos-label
{
   display: block;
   width: 170px;
   float: left;
   margin-bottom: 2px;
}

infos-label
{
   text-align: left;
   width: 95px;
   padding-right: 20px;
   font-weight: bold;
}
```

Let's be More Flexible...

In the example we have been through, we started with the fact that the HTML box would be included directly within the main template. Mochikit comes with a handy DOM toolbox, with functions named after common HTML elements such as DIV, SPAN, INPUT, FORM, etc. It provides an extremely easy way to generate HTML elements on the fly to insert them into the DOM tree held by the browser.

A typical use case of our application will be the presentation of existing albums. Since their number is going to change with time, it is required to generate the associated HTML code dynamically, as shown in the following example:

```
var albumInfoBlock = DIV({'class': 'albums-infos-pane', 'id':
                                  'album-' + album['id']},
                   LABEL({'class': 'infos-label'}, 'Title:'),
                   SPAN({'class': 'infos-content'}, album['title']),
                   LABEL({'class': 'infos-label'}, 'Created on:'),
                   SPAN({'class': 'infos-content'}, album['created']),
```

```
LABEL({'class': 'infos-label'}, 'Updated on:'),
SPAN({'class': 'infos-content'}, album['updated']),
LABEL({'class': 'infos-label'}, 'Description:'),
SPAN({'class': 'infos-content'},
        album['description']));
```

We first create the main block containing the information and then we associate a unique identifier using the pattern `album-#id#`, where `#id#` is the `id` of the album to be displayed. Doing it that way, we provide a unique identifier for each block within the DOM tree. This is required as we will attach mouse events to the block itself for further processing. Then, we attach a series of inline elements, via the `SPAN` element, and we insert the content of the linked attribute of the album.

Once the block is created, we connect the mouse events as follows:

```
connect(albumInfoBlock, 'onclick', selectAlbum);
```

When a user clicks on an album block `selectAlbum` will be called and operations will be performed to display the selected album, as we will see in the next chapter.

Next, we attach the newly created element to an outer album box area and we display it:

```
appendChildNodes(albumsPane, albumInfoBlock);
toggle(albumsPane, 'blind');
```

The creation of the blocks containing the album information will take place in a loop through the albums retrieved from the server, as we will see in the next chapter.

Summary

Through this chapter, we have introduced some of the technologies and tools that are available today to create web application interfaces with dynamic and attractive design.

These range from the good old HTML variants that are still widely used to structure the content, to the CSS, a web designer's best friend to style the interface, and the resourceful Mochikit that lets us step into the world of rich web application.

There is still a missing link to put everything together between the server and the client. This link is commonly referred today as Ajax. This is what we will explain in the next chapter.

8
Ajax

In the previous chapter, we built the photoblog web interface through the use of HTML, DOM, and JavaScript. We have shown how a web page could be modified dynamically from the browser itself. However, we have not detailed the nature of this dynamism, neither have we explained how to retrieve data from a web application server without refreshing the entire web page itself. The one who can do this for us is Ajax. So, the goal of this chapter is to introduce the concept of Ajax.

Rise of the Rich-Client Applications

Until the year 2005, the most common pattern found in web applications was one HTTP request per page. In other words, navigation through a website was done through links that triggered the retrieval through an HTTP request of the linked resource. This pattern is still widely used but competes now with the pattern where we have several HTTP requests per page. The distinction might look anecdotal, but by allowing the browser to issue several HTTP requests to fetch more data from one web page at one given URI, it offers a different yet powerful path to the web developer desirous of creating a more interactive application.

For example, let's imagine a web application that shows a list of results by paging them instead of displaying them all at once. In traditional web applications, each time the end user went forward or backward, a new HTTP request would be sent to the server for the entire page to be reconstructed. In that case, the URL displayed in the browser address bar would also change, based on the current page viewed. On the other hand, imagine that instead of fetching the entire web page, only the new set of data to be displayed was fetched. We would still have one request made each time the customer moves from his or her current position, but it would be done without the replacement of the entire web page. The end user would have a lesser feeling of being governed by web pages, which could improve the overall experience of navigating through the set of data as well as reducing the bandwidth consumption.

This simplistic example is in fact a seed for all kind of enhancements for modern web applications that have led to the rise of rich-client applications.

Ajax

In the year 2005, Jesse James Garrett (http://www.adaptivepath.com/ publications/essays/archives/000385.php) coined the term Ajax to designate a set of technology that he was about to present to one of his clients. It has since then left its original author's hands and is today the referenced term for what we introduced in the previous section about making web applications look more dynamic and interactive.

Ajax stands for **Asynchronous JavaScript and XML**, and covers a set of technologies applied to a web environment. Let's review each part of the acronym:

- **Asynchronous**: In a client-server environment, there are two grand principles; either your operation is running synchronously to the rest of the program or not. If it is, then the program pauses until the operation terminates, and if it is not, then the operation returns immediately and lets the program continue. Once the operation is finished, it informs its main program through a callback function.

  In the context of a web application, the whole purpose of Ajax is to bring more interactivity to the end user, which is why it broadly relies on asynchronous operations. Now, nothing prevents a developer from running specific operations synchronously to the rest of the application. This, however, can lead to the freezing of the entire browser, if the operation is not almost instantaneous.

- **JavaScript**: In a traditional approach where each action from the end user leads to a new HTTP request, this request is generated by the browser itself, which also consumes the HTTP response. With Ajax, the HTTP request is handled by a JavaScript call to an underlying HTTP API that we will review later on. Therefore, the web developer is in charge of creating a valid request, being able to handle its response, and eventually updating the end-user view of the web page.

- **XML**: The main purpose of Ajax is to perform actions on the Document Object Model to either insert new content or remove parts of a web page from the end-user view. Ajax is based on the exchange of XML documents through HTTP. Those documents contain all the information and data necessary to perform the requested operation. Therefore, other formats of information can be used and XML is not compulsory. The most widespread format is JSON, which we will introduce later on.

Ajax—Advantages and Drawbacks

At first sight, the concepts carried by Ajax seem really promising and they certainly are. Nonetheless, the technologies required can lead to unexpected issues. First of all, let's review some of the advantages of Ajax:

- Server and bandwidth usage reduction: In a traditional web application, where each page is requested in its entirety from the server, there is a resource waste from both the server and the network. This is because the server may have to recompute the page and more data is carried on the wire. In both cases, however, the sensible use of caching would decrease that effect.

  When using Ajax principles, only the needed data is fetched from the server. In that case, the server and intermediates could cache it. In any case, Ajax can reduce the load occurring on servers, as part of the processing is moved to the client itself.

- General improvement of the end-user experience: Since the web page view is updated locally on the client side following the user's actions, he or she may feel that the web application is more interactive and more responsive.

- Separation of concerns enforced: Since the web developer is in charge of the construction of the HTTP request to be sent, he or she can decide to actually call different web services based on the current context of the application.

  For instance, in a traditional web application an HTML form would be posted to the web server, which would return an HTML page. Ajax lets the developer decide which service will handle the user input. Therefore, the developer can call an Atom Publishing Protocol service that would return an Atom document that the developer would then handle manually. Ajax web applications can distribute their tasks among different specific services.

Now let's review the drawbacks associated with Ajax:

- One of the biggest issues for web applications, based on the principles of Ajax, is that they by-pass the browser machinery and, therefore, the standard behavior of the backward and forward buttons is not assured anymore. In a more general way, Ajax breaks an end-user habit that has become the standard way of navigating the Web. For instance, the page-to-page pattern is a clear sign that the end-user action has triggered an operation resulting in a modification of the current state of the web page, whereas a web application that will modify only a part of the viewed page can confuse some users.

- Ajax sometimes prevents users from bookmarking the pages.

- Some have raised concerns about the possible security holes brought by Ajax and JavaScript. However, those claims are usually made against applications that had a weak point, not because of JavaScript but because of the way they have designed a functionality. In any case, you should always weigh the potential security risks for your own requirements when using Ajax. For instance, never trust client-side form validation only; make sure you validate any incoming data on the server side and keep client-side validation to minimize round-trip HTTP exchanges.

Generally, the pitfall regarding the use of Ajax in a web application is its overuse. Although this is a fairly subjective topic, the abuse of Ajax is frowned upon when it does not improve the end-user experience as compared to a more traditional approach. Our photoblog application will use Ajax fairly heavily.

Behind the Scene: XMLHttpRequest

As we have seen, Ajax is based on the idea of sending HTTP requests using JavaScript; more specifically Ajax relies on the XMLHttpRequest object and its API to perform those operations. This object was first designed and implemented by Microsoft engineers as an ActiveX control available to Outlook Express and Internet Explorer, but it was not heavily used before the rise of Ajax and rich web applications. XMLHttpRequest is now part of every modern browser and is so widely used that the W3C has notably set up a working group to specify the boundaries of this object to provide the minimum interoperability requirements across implementations.

Let's review the XMLHttpRequest interface specified by W3C, as it provides the most common attributes and functions implemented by browser vendors:

Attributes	Description
readyState	Read-only attribute carrying the current status of the object: 0: Uninitialized 1: Open 2: Sent 3: Receiving 4: Loaded
onreadystatechange	An EventListener is called when the readyState attribute changes.
responseText	Contains the received bytes so far from the server as a string
responseXML	If the content-type of the response was one associated with XML (text/xml, application/xml, or +xml), this contains an instance of the received document.
status	The HTTP response code
statusText	The HTTP response text

Methods	Description
`abort()`	Cancels the underlying network connection with the server.
`getAllReponseHeaders()`	Returns a string of all HTTP response headers separated by a new line.
`getResponseHeader(header)`	Returns the value of the header if present in the response. An empty string otherwise.
`setRequestHeader(header, value)`	Sets an HTTP header for the underlying request.
`open(method, uri, async, user, password)`	Initializes the object: `method`: the HTTP method to be used for the request `uri`: the URI on which the request is applied `async`: a Boolean indicating whether this request must be synchronous with the rest of the program or not `username` and `password`: provide the credentials to access the resource
`send(data)`	Realizes the HTTP connection and sets the request body with data if provided.

The API is fairly straightforward and simple. Let's go through various examples using the MochiKit Async module.

Performing a GET Request

The GET request is as shown:

```
var xmlHttpReq = getXMLHttpRequest();
xmlHttpReq.open("GET", "/", true);

var d = sendXMLHttpRequest(xmlHttpReq);
d.addCallback(function (data)
{
  alert("Success!");
});
d.addErrback(function (data)
{
  alert("An error occurred");
};
```

Now, we will see what we have actually done:

1. As each browser has its own API for the developer who wishes to instantiate an XMLHttpRequest, Mochikit provides the `getXMLHttpRequest()` function that will return the correct object by checking which browser the end user is using.

2. We then initialize the object with required values. In this case, we want to perform a GET request against the "/" URI of the current host in an asynchronous fashion.

3. Then we inform the server that it must close the connection as soon as it finishes with our request and has sent us its response.

4. Then we use the Mochikit `sendXMLHttpRequest()` function that returns a deferred object. This object offers the developer a clean API to handle the different states that an `XMLHttpRequest` object can take during the processing.

   a. We add a callback that will be applied if the response status code indicates a success (typically in the 2xx and 3xx ranges of HTTP).

   b. We also associate an error callback that will be applied when the response indicates an error (typically in the 4xx and 5xx ranges of HTTP).

5. The `data` parameter that each callback must take is the entity body included in the response, which can then be processed by the callback.

Performing a Content-Negotiated GET Request

This GET request is as shown:

```
var xmlHttpReq = getXMLHttpRequest();
xmlHttpReq.open("GET", "/", true);

xmlHttpReq.setRequestHeader('Accept', 'application/atom+xml');
xmlHttpReq.setRequestHeader('Accept-Language', 'fr');
var d = sendXMLHttpRequest(xmlHttpReq);
d.addCallback(function (data)
{
  alert("Success!");
});
d.addErrback(function (data)
{
  alert("An error occured");
});
```

In this request, we inform the server that we are willing to accept content that is represented using the Atom format and which uses the French language. A server that is unable to handle this request could respond with `406 Not Acceptable`, and therefore the error callback would be applied.

Performing a POST Request

The `POST` request is as shown:

```
var qs = queryString(data);
var xmlHttpReq = getXMLHttpRequest();
xmlHttpReq.open("POST", "/album", true);
xmlHttpReq.setRequestHeader('Content-Type',
                            'application/x-www-form-urlencoded');

var d = sendXMLHttpRequest(xmlHttpReq, qs);
d.addCallback(function (data)
{
   // do something
});
d.addErrback(function (data)
{
   // do something else
});
```

Now, we will see what we have actually done:

1. We post some data in the form of an encoded query string. The `queryString(data)` function takes an associative array of key values and returns an encoded string of the form: `key1=value1?key2=value2`.

2. We initialize the `XMLHttpRequest` object.

3. We specify the content-type of our request entity body: `application/x-www-form-urlencoded`

4. Then we request a deferred object from `sendXMLHttpRequest`, but as you can see we also pass the data we wish to send.

Let's POST an XML Document

This is how we will do it:

```
var entry = '<?xml version="1.0" encoding="utf-8"?>
<entry>
  <title>This is my family album</title>
  <id>urn:uuid:25cd2014-2ab3-11db-902d-000ae4ea7d46</id>
  <updated>2006-08-13T11:18:01Z</updated>
```

```
      <content type="text">Some content</content>
    </entry>';
    var xmlHttpReq = getXMLHttpRequest();
    xmlHttpReq.open("POST", "/album", true);
    xmlHttpReq.setRequestHeader('Content-Type', 'application/atom+xml');

    var d = sendXMLHttpRequest(xmlHttpReq, entry);
    d.addCallback(function (data)
    {
      // do something
    });
    d.addErrback(function (data)
    {
      // do something else
    });
```

Performing PUT, HEAD, or DELETE Requests

Unlike HTML forms, XMLHttpRequest is not limited in terms of supported HTTP methods that it recognizes. In fact, XMLHttpRequest does not pay attention to the method that you use and does not interpret it. The method you use is sent as it is to the server. This is extremely important in web services based on REST or the Atom Publishing Protocol, as we have seen in the previous chapters.

Cookies

Cookies are sent along with the request, automatically by the user agent hosting XMLHttpRequest; therefore, there is no specific action for the developer to take.

Authentication using Digest or Basic Schemes

The open() method of XMLHttpRequest can take username and password parameters to be sent along with the request. The authentication schemes supported by XMLHttpRequest are defined in RFC 2617, namely *basic* and *digest*. These two schemes are as follows:

- Basic scheme: The basic scheme is simply the transfer of the username and password encoded using the base64 algorithm. The issue with this is that, if a third-party fetches the encoded value, nothing can be done to prevent it from being decoded. This is why the basic is often referred as sending the password in clear text, because the applied encoding can be decoded very easily. It is therefore not a secure authentication scheme unless it is used on a secured protocol such as HTTPS.

- Digest scheme: The digest scheme, on the other hand, does not send the password as it is across the wire. Instead, both the parties apply the same algorithm using the password and other seeds to compute a digest value of those. The server also sends the seed value on the first request to *tag* that request. The client sends back the computation of the digest algorithm to the server, which compares it with its own computation. If the two match, the request is allowed. This scheme is safer than the basic one, as the password is actually never sent onto the wire in a form that can be decrypted in a reasonable amount of time.

By default, when using those schemes, a browser would open a pop-up window asking for a username and a password. In the context of request issued by a JavaScript call to XMLHttpRequest, it is possible to avoid that pop up by providing the user credentials directly to the open() method. Obviously, it is out of question to hardcode them into the JavaScript code. Instead, it is fairly easy to integrate an HTML form into the web application and to dynamically pass the input values to the JavaScript call, as the following example demonstrates:

```html
<html>
  <head>
    <script type="application/javascript" src="MochiKit/MochiKit.js">
    </script>
    <script type="application/javascript" src="MochiKit/New.js">
    </script>
    <script type="application/javascript">
      doLogin = function()
      {
        // create the XMLHttpRequest object
        var xmlHttpReq = getXMLHttpRequest();
        // initialize the object
        // the "/hello/" + username URI is protected by a password
        // the magic happens here as we pass dynamically the values
        // of the username and password entered by the user
        xmlHttpReq.open("GET", "/hello/" + $("username").value, true,
                          $("username").value, $("password").value);
        // start the request
        var d = sendXMLHttpRequest(xmlHttpReq);
        // let's remove any previous displayed message from the DOM
        replaceChildNodes($("message"));
        // insert a welcome message if the authentication succeeded
        d.addCallback(function (data)
        {
          appendChildNodes($("message"), SPAN({},
                              data.responseText));
```

```
      });
      // insert a message if the authentication failed
      d.addErrback(function (data)
      {
        appendChildNodes($("message"), SPAN({}, "You're not
                                     welcome here."));
      });
    };
  </script>
  <style type="text/css">
  Body
  {
    text-align: center;
    font-family: sans-serif;
  }

  #loginBox
  {
    position:relative;
    margin: 0px auto;
    text-align:left;
    width: 250px;
    color: #2F2F2F;
    padding-top: 25px;
  }

  Fieldset
  {
    background-color: #E9F3FF;
  }

  input, label
  {
    display: block;
    float: left;
    margin-bottom: 2px;
  }

  Label
  {
    text-align: left;
    width: 70px;
    padding-right: 10px;
  }
```

```
    Input
    {
      border: 1px #000 solid;
    }

    #loginButton
    {
      cursor: pointer;
      font-weight: bold;
      text-decoration: none;
      color: #2F2F2F;
    }

    #loginButton:hover
    {
      text-decoration: underline;
    }
    </style>
  </head>
  <body>
    <div id="loginBox">
    <form name="login" id="login">
      <fieldset>
        <label>Username:</label>
        <input type="text" name="username" id="username" />
        <br /><br />
        <label>Password:</label>
        <input type="password" name="password" id="password" />
        <br /><br />
        <span onclick="doLogin();" id="loginButton">Connect</span>
      </fieldset>
    </form>
    </div>
    <div id="message" />
  </body>
</html>
```

The CherryPy script that would serve the previous page could look like:

```
import os.path
import cherrypy

class Root:
  @cherrypy.expose
  def index(self):
```

```
          return file('ajaxdigest.html').read()

    class Hello:
      @cherrypy.expose
      def default(self, username):
        return "Hello %s" % username

    if __name__ == '__main__':
      r = Root()
      r.hello = Hello()
      current_dir = os.path.abspath(os.path.dirname(__file__))

      def get_credentials():
      return {'test': 'test'}

      conf = {'/hello': {'tools.digest_auth.on': True,
                         'tools.digest_auth.realm': 'localhost',
                         'tools.digest_auth.users': get_credentials},
              '/MochiKit': {'tools.staticdir.on': True,
                            'tools.staticdir.dir':
    os.path.join(current_dir, 'MochiKit')}}

      cherrypy.quickstart(r, config=conf)
```

When you access `http://localhost:8080/`, you should get the following page:

If you enter the username `test` and password `test`, you will get the following view on your screen:

On the other hand, if you provide wrong values, you would get a screen like this:

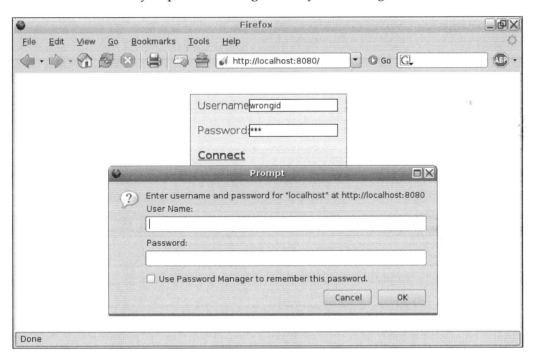

Unfortunately, the browser receives the message from the server about the authentication failure with 401 HTTP error code and handles it itself. As of today, there is no cross-browser way to avoid that issue so that the pop up does not appear. If you hit the **Cancel** button of the pop up, the browser then goes back to your JavaScript code and the error callback is applied.

Moreover, since you cannot access the underlying session through the XMLHttpRequest object as it is handled by the browser, you cannot force a logout by suppressing the session credentials. The user has to close down the browser to disconnect from the application.

Consequently, although XMLHttpRequest allows you to provide a fancier way to enable basic and digest authentication in your web application, there are still some pitfalls that need to be acknowledged.

JSON

As we have already seen in this chapter, in spite of carrying XML in its name, Ajax does not prevent other formats being carried. For instance, one extremely common format that you will see is **JSON (JavaScript Object Notation)**.

In a nutshell, JSON is a way to carry serialized JavaScript objects so that a JavaScript application can evaluate them and transform them into JavaScript objects that the application can manipulate.

For instance, when the user requests the server for an album object formatted with the JSON format, the server would return the following content:

```
{'description': 'This is a simple demo album for you to test',
                                    'author': 'Sylvain'}
```

We then use the evalJSONRequest() function from Mochikit, as follows:

```
var data = evalJSONRequest(incoming);
```

Now the data is a JavaScript associative array and the description field can be accessed via:

```
data['description'];
```

JSON is widely deployed because it is simple, easy to use, and efficient to construct or evaluate. It does support all the common basic types such as numbers, Booleans, arrays, strings, or the null object. More complex objects are translated into associative arrays, where object attribute names serve as keys to access their associated value.

The photoblog application will mainly use the JSON format in its operations.

When your CherryPy application relies heavily on JSON, it may be interesting to write a tool to automatically perform the JSON serialization and deserialization.

```
import cherrypy
import simplejson

def dejsonify(encoding='utf-8'):
  if cherrypy.request.method in ['POST', 'PUT']:
    if 'content-type' in cherrypy.request.headers:
      if cherrypy.request.headers['content-type'] ==
                                'application/json':
        body_as_dict = simplejson.loads(
                      cherrypy.request.body.read())
        for key in body_as_dict:
          cherrypy.request.params[key.encode(encoding)] =
                                body_as_dict[key]

def jsonify():
  if isinstance(cherrypy.response.body, dict):
    cherrypy.response.headers['Content-Type'] = 'application/json'
      cherrypy.response.body = simplejson.dumps(
                  cherrypy.response.body)

cherrypy.tools.dejsonifier = cherrypy.Tool('before_handler',
                                          dejsonify)
cherrypy.tools.jsonifier = cherrypy.Tool('before_finalize', jsonify)

class Root:
  def index(self):
    return {'message': 'Hello'}
  index.exposed = True

  def process(self, name):
    # do something here
    return "Processed %s" % name
  process.exposed = True

if __name__ == '__main__':
  conf = {'/': {'tools.dejsonifier.on': True,
                'tools.jsonifier.on': True}}
  cherrypy.quickstart(Root(), config=conf)
```

We create two tools using the simple JSON module to perform the conversion. The first one deserializes the request body from JSON only on POST and PUT requests that have the `application/json` content-type set. The tool loads the request body and transforms it into a dictionary, which is thereafter injected in the `params` attribute of the `cherrypy.request` object allowing CherryPy page handlers to expect keys of the JSON dictionary as regular parameters, as you can see in the process page handler. Note that we must encode those keys into Python strings from Unicode because CherryPy page handlers expect strings.

The second tool takes the dictionary returned by a page handler and serializes it into JSON.

Applying Ajax to our Application

Our photoblog application will use Ajax fairly extensively, and to explain this we will review how to handle the albums of the photoblog.

Defining the Required Namespaces

Our first step will be to define the JavaScript namespaces that will allow us to reuse common function names in different contexts while avoiding name collision. Using the term namespace is slightly unexpected because JavaScript does not have that notion per se, but it is possible to emulate this feature in a number of ways. In the case of this application, we will be using JavaScript inheritance that is simple enough to implement our requirement.

The two namespaces that the photoblog application will use are: `ui` and `services`.

The `ui` namespace will cover the different interactions with the end user, while the `services` namespace will take care of exchanging data with the server. The `ui` namespace classes and functions will therefore call the `services` ones to perform operations requested by the end user.

To implement these two namespaces, we will simply define two empty JavaScript functions as follows:

```
function service()
{
};

function ui()
{
};
```

Implementing Namespaces

We now have our functions and we can add attributes to them. Here we have the album class declaration that will handle all aspects of the album entity from a client-side point of view:

```
function albums()
{
  this.visibility = false;
  this.current = null;
  this.position = 0;
  this.step = 3;
};

ui.prototype.albums = new albums();
var ui = new ui();
```

Here, we first create a regular JavaScript function that is used as the constructor of an album class. We also declare a few attributes attached to that object via the JavaScript keyword this.

Then we add an albums instance as an attribute of the ui function object prototype and we finally create the unique instance of the ui class that we will use throughout the life of the application within the session of the user.

From now on we can use the albums instance to call its edit method:

```
ui.albums.edit(...)
```

We then define similarly the album class within the services namespace.

```
function album()
{
};
service.prototype.albums = new album();
var services = new service();
```

Adding Methods to the Classes

The first method that we will add to our classes will be the one that toggles the visibility state of our albums container. This container will display information about existing albums and will fade in or fade out when the user clicks on the associated link. Let's see how to add methods:

```
albums.prototype.toggle = function(event)
{
  toggle($('content-pane'), 'blind');
```

```
    if(this.visibility == false)
    {
      this.visibility = true;
      this.forward(e);
    }
    Else
    {
      this.visibility = false;
      replaceChildNodes(albumsPane);
    }
    toggle($('albums-pane'), 'blind');
  };
```

This method first toggles the visibility of the content panel that contains the current photograph. Then if the toggle means to open the `albums` panel, we set its visibility to `true` and we call the `forward` method. Otherwise, we set the visibility to `false` and we delete any elements attached to that container so that they don't waste memory. Finally, we request Mochikit to change the visibility state of the `albums` panel. We then connect that method to the `onclick` signal of the associated link as follows:

```
connect($('albums'), 'onclick', ui.albums, 'toggle');
```

The `forward` method is defined as follows:

```
albums.prototype.forward = function(event)
{
  var start = this.position;
  var end = start + this.step;
  services.albums.fetch_range(start, end, this);
  this.position = end;
};
```

The method first defines the range of albums we will need to fetch from the server. Then we call the `fetch_range()` method of the `services.albums` object, and we finally set the new starting position for the next call to that method.

Let's now review the `services.albums` object itself:

```
album.prototype.fetch_range = function(start, end, src)
{
  var xmlHttpReq = getXMLHttpRequest();
  xmlHttpReq.open("GET", albumsBaseUri.concat(start, "-", end), true);

  xmlHttpReq.setRequestHeader('Accept', 'application/json');
  var d = sendXMLHttpRequest(xmlHttpReq);
```

```
    d.addCallback(function (data)
{
        var data = evalJSONRequest(data);
        src.populate(data);
    });
};
```

You may notice that this method takes an extra parameter named `src`, which is the calling object so that our callbacks can apply methods on that object when receiving a response from the server.

The requested URI `albumsBaseUri.concat(start, "-", end). albumsBaseUri,` is a global string variable containing the base URI for performing requests against collections of albums.

We specify that we would prefer the server to send us back a JSON content, as this is what we will be using to populate the retrieved albums.

The request issued would look like this:

```
http://localhost:8080/services/rest/albums/0-3

GET /services/rest/albums/0-3 HTTP/1.1
Host: localhost:8080
Accept: application/json
Connection: close
```

And its response would be:

```
HTTP/1.x 200 OK
Connection: close
Date: Tue, 19 Sep 2006 20:29:07 GMT
Content-Length: 763
Content-Type: application/json
Allow: GET, HEAD
Server: CherryPy/3.0.0beta
```

The returned content would be then evaluated by the MochiKit function `evalJSONRequest()` to return an instance of JavaScript objects; in this case an array of associative arrays. Once we have received and evaluated the content, we call the `populate()` method of the `ui.album` class to display the retrieved albums. This method is defined as follows:

```
albums.prototype.populate = function(albums)
{
  // get the albums container
  var albumsPane = $('albums-pane');
```

```
// we remove any already displayed albums form the DOM tree
replaceChildNodes($('albums-pane'));

// define a set of links that we will use to move through the
// set of albums
var previous = SPAN({'id': 'previous-albums', 'class':
                          'infos-action'}, 'Previous');
connect(previous, 'onclick', this, 'rewind');

var next = SPAN({'id': 'next-albums', 'class': 'infos-action'},
                                            'Next');
connect(next, 'onclick', this, 'forward');

// we also add a link that when triggered will display the
// form to create a new Album
var create = SPAN({'class': 'infos-action'}, 'Create');
connect(create, 'onclick',this, 'blank');

// in case no albums were retrieved we simply display a default
// message
if(albums.length == 0)
{
  appendChildNodes(albumsPane, SPAN({'id': 'info-msg', 'class':
                        'info-msg'}, 'No more album to view.'));
  appendChildNodes(albumsPane, previous);
  return;
}

// now we traverse the array of retrieved albums to construct
// a tree structure of each that we will then insert into the
// main DOM tree
for(var album in albums)
{
  album = albums[album];
  var albumInfoBlock = DIV({'class': 'albums-infos-pane', 'id':
                                        'album-' + album['id']},
  LABEL({'class': 'infos-label'}, 'Title:'),
  SPAN({'class': 'infos-content'}, album['title']), BR(),
  LABEL({'class': 'infos-label'}, 'Created on:'),
  SPAN({'class': 'infos-content'}, album['created']), BR(),
  LABEL({'class': 'infos-label'}, 'Updated on:'),
  SPAN({'class': 'infos-content'}, album['modified']), BR(),
  LABEL({'class': 'infos-label'}, 'Description:'),
  SPAN({'class': 'infos-content'}, album['description']), BR());
```

```
// we provide a link Edit and Delete to each album displayed

var editAlbumElement = SPAN({'class': 'infos-action'}, 'Edit');
connect(editAlbumElement, 'onclick', this, 'fetch_for_edit');
var deleteAlbumElement = SPAN({'class': 'infos-action'},
                             'Delete');
connect(deleteAlbumElement, 'onclick', this, 'ditch');

appendChildNodes(albumInfoBlock, editAlbumElement);
appendChildNodes(albumInfoBlock, deleteAlbumElement);

// we finally connect the onclick signal of the block
// carrying the album information. When a user clicks
// it will toggle the albums panel visibility and
// display the selected album.
connect(albumInfoBlock, 'onclick', this, 'select');
appendChildNodes(albumsPane, albumInfoBlock); .
}

// we eventually insert all those new elements into the
// main DOM tree to be displayed.
appendChildNodes(albumsPane, previous);
appendChildNodes(albumsPane, next);
appendChildNodes(albumsPane, create);
};
```

Method to Create a New Album

Now that we can display albums, we will review how to create a new album.
To do so, we first need a form to gather the user input. Let's explain the
`ui.albums.blank()` method that is in charge of displaying the form by dynamically
inserting it into the DOM tree.

```
albums.prototype.blank = function(e)
{
  // those two elements will be links to either submit the form
  // or canceling the process by closing the form
  var submitLink = SPAN({'id': 'form-submit', 'class': 'form-link'},
                                                    'Submit');
  var cancelLink = SPAN({'id': 'form-cancel', 'class': 'form-link'},
                                                    'Cancel');

  // we will insert error messages when specific fields are
  // not filled
```

```
    var successMessage = SPAN({'id': 'form-success', 'class':
                              'form-success'}, 'Album created');
    var errorMessage = SPAN({'id': 'form-error', 'class':
            'form-error'}, 'An unexpected error occured');
    var titleErrMsg = SPAN({'id': 'form-title-error', 'class':
                    'form-error'}, 'You must provide a title');
    var authorErrMsg = SPAN({'id': 'form-author-error', 'class':
            'form-error'}, 'You must specify the author name');
    var descErrMsg = SPAN({'id': 'form-desc-error', 'class':
            'form-error'}, 'You must provide a description');

    // the main form
    var albumForm = DIV({'id': 'pageoverlay'},
        DIV({'id': 'outerbox'},
        DIV({'id': 'formoverlay'},
        SPAN({'class': 'form-caption'}, 'Create a new album'),
        BR(),BR(),
        FORM({'id': 'create-album', 'name':"albumForm"}, titleErrMsg,
        LABEL({'class': 'form-label'}, 'Title:'),
        INPUT({'class': 'form-input', 'name': 'title', 'id':
                              'album-title', 'value': ''}),
        BR(),
        LABEL({'class': 'form-label'}, 'Segment:'),
        INPUT({'class': 'form-input', 'name': 'segment', 'id':
            'album-segment', 'value': ''}), BR(), authorErrMsg,
        LABEL({'class': 'form-label'}, 'Author:'),
        INPUT({'class': 'form-input', 'name': 'author', 'id':
              'album-author', 'value': ''}), BR(), descErrMsg,
        LABEL({'class': 'form-label'}, 'Description:'),
        TEXTAREA({'class': 'form-textarea', 'name': 'description',
              'id': 'album-desc', 'rows': '2', 'value': ''}), BR(),
        LABEL({'class': 'form-label'}, 'Content:'),
        TEXTAREA({'class': 'form-textarea', 'name': 'content', 'id':
                  'album-content', 'rows': '7', 'value': ''}), BR()),
        successMessage, errorMessage,
        DIV({'id': 'form-links'},
        submitLink,
        cancelLink))));

    hideElement(titleErrMsg);
    hideElement(authorErrMsg);
    hideElement(descErrMsg);
    hideElement(errorMessage);
    hideElement(successMessage);
```

```
    connect(submitLink, 'onclick', this, 'create');
    connect(cancelLink, 'onclick', closeOverlayBox);
    appendChildNodes($('photoblog'), albumForm);
};
```

The creation of the form block requires further explanation. In order to provide a fancier panel carrying the form, we use the technique deployed in scripts such as *Lightbox* or *Thickbox*. Both rely on the overlay capabilities of CSS applied to the DOM to display elements on top of others. Overlays allow displaying elements not in a sequential fashion but as a pile. This feature associated with a sensible use of HTML blocks as DIVs and appropriate colors can provide an attractive way to display the content, as the following screenshot demonstrates:

If you do not fill the required fields and submit the form, you will end up with a screen as displayed in the following screenshot:

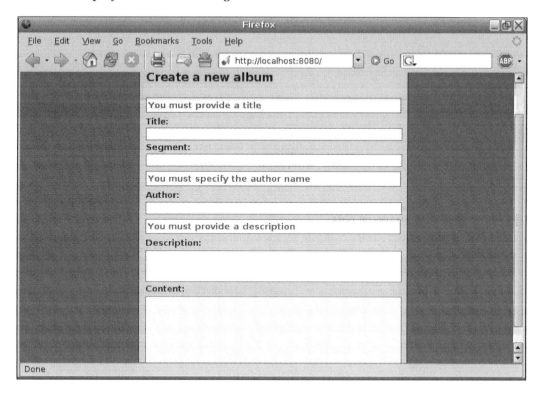

If you fill the required fields and submit the form, you would get a screen as shown:

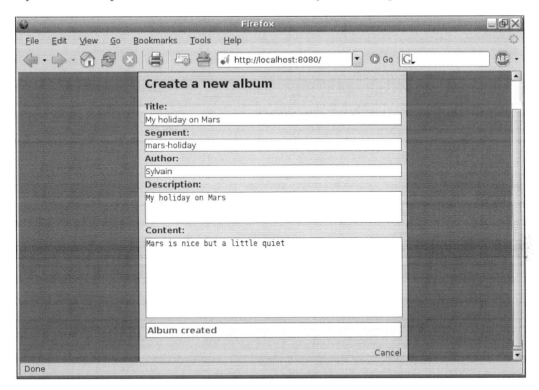

In order to avoid the situation where the user tries to re-submit the form, we remove the **Submit** link and the user can now safely close this screen.

The HTTP exchange will look like this:

```
POST /services/rest/album/ HTTP/1.1
Host: localhost:8080
Accept: application/json
Accept-Language: en-us,en;q=0.5
Accept-Encoding: gzip,deflate
Accept-Charset: ISO-8859-1,utf-8;q=0.7,*;q=0.7

Content-Type: application/x-www-form-urlencoded
Content-Length: 167
Pragma: no-cache

blog_id=1&title=My%20holiday%20on%20Mars&author=Sylvain&description=
My%20holiday%20on%20Mars.&content=Mars%20is%20nice%20but%20a%20little
%20quiet.

HTTP/1.x 201 Created
```

```
Connection: close
Content-Length: 289
Server: CherryPy/3.0.0beta
Location: http://localhost:8080/album/19
Allow: DELETE, GET, HEAD, POST, PUT
Date: Wed, 20 Sep 2006 19:59:59 GMT
```

Note that the response gives us the URI to directly access the newly created album.

The method to handle the previous HTTP exchange is `services.album.create()`, as follows:

```
album.prototype.create = function(data, src)
{
  var qs = queryString(data);
  var xmlHttpReq = getXMLHttpRequest();
  xmlHttpReq.open("POST", albumBaseUri, true);
  xmlHttpReq.setRequestHeader('Content-Type',
        'application/x-www-form-urlencoded');

  xmlHttpReq.setRequestHeader('Accept', 'application/json');
  var d = sendXMLHttpRequest(xmlHttpReq, qs);
  d.addCallback(function (data)
  {
    src.showSuccessMessage();
  });
  d.addErrback(function (data)
  {
    src.showErrorMessage();
  });
};
```

The `data` parameter is a JavaScript associative array of the form fields. The `src` parameter is the `ui.albums` instance, which is extended with the following methods:

```
albums.prototype.create = function(event)
{
  if(this.validate())
  {
    // blogId is a global variable containing the current photoblog
    // identifier
    var data = {'blog_id': blogId, 'title': $('album-title').value,
                'author': album-author').value,
                'description': $('album-desc').value,
                'content': $('album-content').value};
```

```
      services.albums.create(data, this);
   }
};

albums.prototype.validate = function()
{
   var ready = true;
   hideElement($('form-title-error'));
   hideElement($('form-author-error'));
   hideElement($('form-desc-error'));

   if($('album-title').value == '')
   {
      appear($('form-title-error'));
      ready = false;
   }

   if($('album-author').value == '')
   {
      appear($('form-author-error'));
      ready = false;
   }

   if($('album-desc').value == '')
   {
      appear($('form-desc-error'));
      ready = false;
   }

   return ready;
};

albums.prototype.showSuccessMessage = function()
{
   hideElement($('form-title-error'));
   hideElement($('form-author-error'));
   hideElement($('form-desc-error'));

   appear($('form-success'));
   fade($('form-submit'));
};
albums.prototype.showErrorMessage = function()
{
     hideElement($('form-title-error'));
     hideElement($('form-author-error'));
```

```
    hideElement($('form-desc-error'));

    appear($('form-error'));
};
```

Method to Update an Existing Album

This follows the same principles as we have seen in the previous section, except that we provide an album object to fill the form automatically with its values.

Method to Delete an Existing Album

Finally, we need a method to delete an album:

```
// method part of the ui namespace
albums.prototype.ditch = function(event)
{
  // stop the propagation of the click event so that
  // the select method is not applied
  event.stop();
  // shows a modal dialogbox asking the confirmation of the deletion
  var doit = confirm("Are you sure you want to delete this album?");
  if(doit)
  {
    // we retrieve the id of the album to delete from
    // the block carrying the album <div id="album-19">...</div>
    var currentAlbumId = (e.src().parentNode.id).substr(6);
    services.albums.remove(currentAlbumId);
    switchOff(e.src().parentNode);
  }
};


// method part of the services namespace
album.prototype.remove = function(id)
{
  if(id != null)
  {
    var xmlHttpReq = getXMLHttpRequest();
    xmlHttpReq.open("DELETE", albumBaseUri + id, true);

    var d = sendXMLHttpRequest(xmlHttpReq);
  }
};
```

The HTTP exchange would look like this:

```
DELETE /services/rest/album/19 HTTP/1.1
Host: localhost:8080
Connection: close
Content-Length: 0

HTTP/1.x 200 OK
Connection: close
Date: Wed, 20 Sep 2006 20:39:49 GMT
Content-Length: 0
Allow: DELETE, GET, HEAD, POST, PUT
Server: CherryPy/3.0.0beta
```

We have explained the basic methods to manipulate albums of the photoblog application. The same principles will be applied for the other entities of the application: film and photo.

Summary

This chapter has introduced you to Ajax and more generally to the basics of client-side programming using JavaScript. The possibilities are almost endless and the near future should see extremely interesting and powerful web applications that will slowly take the place of their rich-client counterparts.

9
Testing

Until now, we have reviewed the different steps involved in building the photoblog application but we have not tested our design and implementation. This chapter will introduce some testing techniques such as unit, functional, and load testing using open-source products such as unittest, CherryPy webtest, FunkLoad, and Selenium. By the end of this chapter, you should have a good understanding of how to use these tools in their context and improve the test suite for your applications.

Why Testing

Why testing, some might wonder? Does it bring any value to the application? You may believe that if a problem is found in your code, it will be reported and eventually be fixed. Therefore, you may argue that testing is fairly irrelevant and is time consuming. If you do believe this, then with the help of this chapter we will try to show you that testing is not just the cherry on the cake but actually it is part of the recipe for success.

Testing is a process during which the application is audited from different perspectives in order to:

- Find bugs
- Find differences between the expected and real result, output, states, etc.
- Understand how complete the implementation is
- Exercise the application in realistic situations before its release

The goal of testing is not to put the developer at fault but to provide tools to estimate the health of the application at a given time. Testing measures the quality of an application.

Testing is, therefore, not just a part of the application life cycle but is actually the true barometer of where the application stands in that cycle. Lines of code are meaningless; but test summary and test reports are the reference points that the different members of a project can relate to for understanding what has been achieved, what still needs to be achieved, and how to plan it.

Planning a Test

From the previous section we can say that since testing is so critical to a project, everything should be tested and reviewed. This is true, but it does not mean the same amount of resources and efforts should be allocated to every part of the system under test.

First of all, it depends on the position of the project in its life cycle. For instance, there is little need for performance testing right at the beginning of the project. There might not be a need for capacity testing, if the application does not require lots of hardware or network resources. That being said some tests will be carried all along the life cycle of the project. They will be built up by successive iterations bringing more strength to the test each time.

To summarize, testing needs to be planned in advance in order to define:

- Goals: What is it relevant to test and for what purpose?
- Scope: What is in the scope of the test? What is not?
- Requirements: What will the test involve in terms of resources (human, software, hardware, etc.)?
- Risks: What are the risks related to that test if it does not pass? What will be the mitigation and action taken? Will it stop the project? What is the impact?

These are just a few points to be kept in mind while planning a test.

Another important point is that testing does not end once the application is released. It can also be carried on later so that the production release meets the defined requirements. In any case, since testing draws together so many different aspects it should be seen as a long, continuous process.

Common Testing Approach

Testing is a generic term for a range of aspects to be validated on a system or application. Here is a brief list of the common ones:

- Unit testing: Usually carried by the developers themselves. Unit tests aim at checking whether a unit of code works as expected.

- Usability testing: Developers may usually forget that they are writing an application for end users who do not have knowledge of the system and might end up making it unusable. Functional and usability tests provide a way to make sure that applications will fulfill user expectations.

- Functional/Acceptance testing: While usability testing checks whether the application or system is usable, functional testing ensures that every specified functionality is implemented.

- Load and performance testing: Once an application or system has reached a certain level of completeness, it may require load and performance tests to be conducted in order to understand whether the system can cope with its expected peak load and to find potential bottlenecks. This can lead to changing hardware, optimizing SQL queries, etc.

- Regression testing: Regression testing verifies that successive releases of a product do not break any of the previously working functionalities. Unit testing can be considered as a part of regression testing in some ways.

- Reliability and resilience testing: Some applications or systems cannot afford to break at any time. Reliability and resilience tests can validate how the system application copes with the breakdown of one or several components.

The previous list is far from being exhaustive and each system or application environment may require specific types of testing to be defined.

Unit Testing

Our photoblog application will extensively use unit tests in order to constantly check the following:

- New functionalities work correctly and as expected.

- Existing functionalities are not broken by new code release.

- Defects are fixed and remain fixed.

Python comes in with a standard `unittest` module and also provides a `doctest` module offering a different approach to unit testing as we will explain later on.

unittest

unittest is rooted in JUnit, a Java unit test package developed by Kent Beck and Erich Gamma, which in turn came from a Smalltalk testing framework developed by Kent Beck. Let's now review a basic example of this module.

Unit tests can often work on mock objects that are so called because they support the same interface as the domain objects of the applications but do not actually perform any work. They simply return defined data. Mock objects therefore allow testing against an interface of our design without having to rely on the overall application to be deployed for instance. They also provide a way to run tests in isolation mode from other tests.

First let's define a dummy class as follows:

```
class Dummy:
    def __init__(self, start=0, left_boundary=-10, right_boundary=10,
                 allow_positive=True, allow_negative=False):
        self.current = start
        self.left_boundary = left_boundary
        self.right_boundary = right_boundary
        self.allow_positive = allow_positive
        self.allow_negative = allow_negative

    def forward(self):
        next = self.current + 1
        if (next > 0) and (not self.allow_positive):
            raise ValueError, "Positive values are not allowed"
        if next > self.right_boundary:
            raise ValueError, "Right boundary reached"
        self.current = next
        return self.current

    def backward(self):
        prev = self.current - 1
        if (prev < 0) and (not self.allow_negative):
            raise ValueError, "Negative values are not allowed"
        if prev < self.left_boundary:
            raise ValueError, "Left boundary reached"
        self.current = prev
        return self.current

    def __str__(self):
        return str(self.current)

    def __repr__(self):
        return "Dummy object at %s" % hex(id(self))
```

This class provides an interface to get the next or previous value within a range defined by the left and right boundaries. We could imagine it as a mock object of a more complex class but providing dummy data.

A simple usage of this class is as follows:

```
>>> from dummy import Dummy
>>> dummy = Dummy()
>>> dummy.forward()
1
>>> dummy.forward()
2
>>> dummy.backward()
1
>>> dummy.backward()
0
>>> dummy.backward()
Traceback (most recent call last):
  File "<stdin>", line 1, in ?
  File "dummy.py", line 27, in backward
    raise ValueError, "Negative values are not allowed"
ValueError: Negative values are not allowed
```

Let's imagine we wish to unit test this exciting module to make sure that the code is correct.

```
import unittest

class DummyTest(unittest.TestCase):
    def test_01_forward(self):
        dummy = Dummy(right_boundary=3)
        self.assertEqual(dummy.forward(), 1)
        self.assertEqual(dummy.forward(), 2)
        self.assertEqual(dummy.forward(), 3)
        self.assertRaises(ValueError, dummy.forward)

    def test_02_backward(self):
        dummy = Dummy(left_boundary=-3, allow_negative=True)
        self.assertEqual(dummy.backward(), -1)
        self.assertEqual(dummy.backward(), -2)
        self.assertEqual(dummy.backward(), -3)
        self.assertRaises(ValueError, dummy.backward)

    def test_03_boundaries(self):
        dummy = Dummy(right_boundary=3, left_boundary=-3,
                      allow_negative=True)
```

```
        self.assertEqual(dummy.backward(), -1)
        self.assertEqual(dummy.backward(), -2)
        self.assertEqual(dummy.forward(), -1)
        self.assertEqual(dummy.backward(), -2)
        self.assertEqual(dummy.backward(), -3)
        self.assertRaises(ValueError, dummy.backward)
        self.assertEqual(dummy.forward(), -2)
        self.assertEqual(dummy.forward(), -1)
        self.assertEqual(dummy.forward(), 0)
        self.assertEqual(dummy.backward(), -1)
        self.assertEqual(dummy.forward(), 0)
        self.assertEqual(dummy.forward(), 1)
        self.assertEqual(dummy.forward(), 2)
```

Let's explain this code step by step:

1. To provide unit test capabilities using the `unittest` standard module you only need to import that specific module.

2. Create a class that subclasses `unittest.TestCase`, which is the interface providing unit test functionalities to our code. This class is referred to as a **test case**.

3. Create methods starting with the word `test`. Each method starting with it will be called by the `unittest` internal handler. Notice that the methods this class defines also use a two-digit pattern. This is not required by `unittest` but it allows us to force methods to be called in the order we wish. Indeed `unittest` calls methods by alpha-numeric order, which can sometimes lead to unexpected results. Providing digits like this is a good way to work around that limitation.

4. Call the different `assert`/`fail` methods provided by the `TestCase` class to perform checking of values, exceptions, outputs, etc.

The next step is to run this test case as follows:

```
if __name__ == '__main__':
    unittest.main()
```

This assumes that the call to `main()` is done from within the same module containing the `TestCase` class. The result of this test looks like the following:

```
...
-----------------------------------------------------------------
Ran 3 tests in 0.000s

OK
```

It is common to make the output a little more verbose as follows:

```
if __name__ == '__main__':
    unittest.main(testRunner=unittest.TextTestRunner(verbosity=2))
```

This will produce the following output:

```
test_01_forward (__main__.DummyTest) ... ok
test_02_backward (__main__.DummyTest) ... ok
test_03_boundaries (__main__.DummyTest) ... ok

----------------------------------------------------------------------
Ran 3 tests in 0.000s

OK
```

Now let's provoke an error so that one of the tests fails. In test_01_forward replace the first assertEqual with the following:

```
self.assertEqual(dummy.forward(), 0)
```

Then while running the test again you should get the following output:

```
test_01_forward (__main__.DummyTest) ... FAIL
test_02_backward (__main__.DummyTest) ... ok
test_03_boundaries (__main__.DummyTest) ... ok

======================================================================
FAIL: test_01_forward (__main__.DummyTest)
----------------------------------------------------------------------
Traceback (most recent call last):
  File "dummy.py", line 54, in test_01_forward
    self.assertEqual(dummy.forward(), 0)
AssertionError: 1 != 0

----------------------------------------------------------------------
Ran 3 tests in 0.001s

FAILED (failures=1)
```

As you can see, the unittest module does not stop processing any remaining test cases when one fails. Instead, it displays the traceback of the raised assertion error. Here the test is wrong but in the case where your assertion is a valid one, it would point to a failure of your application.

Let's assume that we write a test that tries to go forward when the right boundary is less than the starting point. We assume that the documentation of the method tells us that it should raise an exception expressing the fact that the class has rejected this case.

Let's create `test_00_construct` accordingly:

```
def test_00_construct(self):
    self.assertRaises(ValueError, Dummy, start=34)
```

Let's run the test now:

```
test_00_construct (__main__.DummyTest) ... FAIL
test_01_forward (__main__.DummyTest) ... ok
test_02_backward (__main__.DummyTest) ... ok
test_03_boundaries (__main__.DummyTest) ... ok


======================================================================
FAIL: test_00_construct (__main__.DummyTest)
----------------------------------------------------------------------
Traceback (most recent call last):
  File "dummy.py", line 50, in test_00_construct
    self.assertRaises(ValueError, Dummy, start=34)
AssertionError: ValueError not raised


----------------------------------------------------------------------
Ran 4 tests in 0.003s

FAILED (failures=1)
```

As you can see the test case does fail on the new test we have included. The reason is that the `Dummy.__init__()` method does not contain any error handling for this case unlike what the documentation told us. Let's fix this by adding the following code at the bottom of the `__init__` method:

```
if (start > right_boundary) or (start < left_boundary):
    raise ValueError, "Start point must belong to the boundaries"
```

Let's now re-run the test:

```
test_00_construct (__main__.DummyTest) ... ok
test_01_forward (__main__.DummyTest) ... ok
test_02_backward (__main__.DummyTest) ... ok
test_03_boundaries (__main__.DummyTest) ... ok


----------------------------------------------------------------------
Ran 4 tests in 0.000s

OK
```

The previous example shows that it is sometimes desirable to write the test before implementing the functionality itself in order to avoid designing the test to match the code behavior. This is often called test-driven development. Another way to achieve this is to provide the API of the application or library to a third party, who will write the test case based on that API in a neutral fashion. Either way the previous example demonstrates that unit testing is only relevant when the tests are coherent with the design and are there to test the implementation.

Now that we have introduced the `unittest` module let's present the `doctest` one.

doctest

The `doctest` module supports running Python code inlined within an object docstring. The advantage of this technique is that test cases are close to the code they test. The inconvenience is that some complex tests can be difficult to achieve this way. Let's see an example on the class we have defined earlier.

```
class Dummy:
    def __init__(self, start=0, left_boundary=-10, right_boundary=10,
                 allow_positive=True, allow_negative=False):
        """
        >>> dummy = Dummy(start=27)
        Traceback (most recent call last):
          ...
            raise ValueError, "Start point must belong to the
                              boundaries"
        ValueError: Start point must belong to the boundaries
        >>> dummy = Dummy()
        >>> dummy.backward()
        Traceback (most recent call last):
          ...
            raise ValueError, "Negative values are not allowed"
        ValueError: Negative values are not allowed

        """
        self.current = start
        self.left_boundary = left_boundary
        self.right_boundary = right_boundary
        self.allow_positive = allow_positive
        self.allow_negative = allow_negative

        if (start > right_boundary) or (start < left_boundary):
            raise ValueError, "Start point must belong to the
                              boundaries"
```

```
def forward(self):
    """

    >>> dummy = Dummy(right_boundary=3)
    >>> dummy.forward()
    1
    >>> dummy.forward()
    2
    >>> dummy.forward()
    3
    >>> dummy.forward()
    Traceback (most recent call last):
      ...
        raise ValueError, "Right boundary reached"
    ValueError: Right boundary reached

    """
    next = self.current + 1
    if (next > 0) and (not self.allow_positive):
        raise ValueError, "Positive values are not allowed"
    if next > self.right_boundary:
        raise ValueError, "Right boundary reached"
    self.current = next
    return self.current
def backward(self):
    """

    >>> dummy = Dummy(left_boundary=-3, allow_negative=True)
    >>> dummy.forward()
    1
    >>> dummy.backward()
    0
    >>> dummy.backward()
    -1
    >>> dummy.backward()
    -2
    >>> dummy.backward()
    -3
    >>> dummy.backward()
    Traceback (most recent call last):
      ...
        raise ValueError, "Left boundary reached"
    ValueError: Left boundary reached

    """
    prev = self.current - 1
```

```
        if (prev < 0) and (not self.allow_negative):
            raise ValueError, "Negative values are not allowed"
        if prev < self.left_boundary:
            raise ValueError, "Left boundary reached"
        self.current = prev
        return self.current

    def __str__(self):
        return str(self.current)

    def __repr__(self):
        return "Dummy object at %s" % hex(id(self))
```

As you can see, each method you wish to test must have a docstring containing use cases that will be run as-is by the `doctest` module.

Then you can run the test as follows:

```
if __name__ == '__main__':
    doctest.testmod()

sylvain@6[test]$ python dummy.py -v
Trying:
    dummy = Dummy(start=27)
Expecting:
    Traceback (most recent call last):
      ...
        raise ValueError, "Start point must belong to the boundaries"
    ValueError: Start point must belong to the boundaries
ok
Trying:
    dummy = Dummy()
Expecting nothing
ok
Trying:
    dummy.backward()
Expecting:
    Traceback (most recent call last):
      ...
        raise ValueError, "Negative values are not allowed"
    ValueError: Negative values are not allowed
ok
Trying:
    dummy = Dummy(left_boundary=-3, allow_negative=True)
```

```
Expecting nothing
ok
Trying:
    dummy.forward()
Expecting:
    1
ok
```

We do not reproduce the complete result trace as it is too long for the purpose of the chapter. You may consider that mixing code and documentation will reduce the efficiency of both, making the documentation harder to read. This concern is actually raised by the `doctest` module documentation itself, which sensibly advises handling *docstring examples with care*. Indeed, since the code belongs to the docstring, it will be displayed while viewing it.

```
>>> from dummy import Dummy
>>> help(Dummy.forward)
Help on method forward in module dummy:

forward(self) unbound dummy.Dummy method
    >>> dummy = Dummy(right_boundary=3)
    >>> dummy.forward()
    1
    >>> dummy.forward()
    2
    >>> dummy.forward()
    3
    >>> dummy.forward()
    Traceback (most recent call last):
      ...
        raise ValueError, "Right boundary reached"
    ValueError: Right boundary reached
```

In such cases the tests can either be part of the documentation itself or be too complex making the documentation unusable.

In a nutshell both the `unittest` and `doctest` modules deserve to be reviewed for your requirements and it is common to find both being used in a single project to provide a strong unit-test suite. In any case, we recommend you to read the documentation of both the modules, which will demonstrate that there is much more than the brief introduction given in this chapter. In addition a very informative mailing-list is available at `http://lists.idyll.org/listinfo/testing-in-python`.

Unit Testing Web Applications

In the previous section, we have presented two standard modules to perform unit testing in Python applications and packages. Unfortunately as they stand they lack some common features to help in specific contexts such as web applications. The Python community has obviously come up with solutions and there are several good extensions to unittest or completely distinct test packages to help us.

We will use an extension to unittest, provided by CherryPy, called webtest and developed by Robert Brewer.

This module provides a transparent integration with CherryPy and also provides a command-line helper to test different configurations of servers. It allows a test to be stopped when a failure occurs, offers access to the HTTP stack when an error is raised, also supports code coverage and profiling, etc. In a nutshell this module starts a CherryPy server automatically, which each test case uses to mount CherryPy applications as needed for the test run and to perform HTTP requests on that server.

This section will now show all the different test cases of our photoblog application but you will find them within the source code of the application. Based on what we have explained in the previous section we design our test cases as follows:

```python
class TestServicesREST(PhotoblogTest):
    def test_00_REST(self):
        self.getPage("/services/rest/")
        self.assertStatus(404)

        self.getPage("/services/rest/album/", method="XYU")
        self.assertStatus(405)

    def test_02_REST_GET(self):
        # missing the ID
        self.getPage("/services/rest/album/")
        self.assertStatus(400)

        # missing the Accept header
        self.getPage("/services/rest/album/2")
        self.assertStatus(406)

        # wrong ID type
        self.getPage("/services/rest/album/st",
                    headers=[("Accept", "application/json")])
        self.assertStatus(404)
```

```python
        self.getPage("/services/rest/album/2",
                    headers=[("Accept", "application/json")])
        self.assertStatus(200)
        self.assertHeader('Content-Type', 'application/json')
        self.assertHeader('Allow', 'DELETE, GET, HEAD, POST, PUT')

        self.getPage("/services/rest/album?album_id=2",
                    headers=[("Accept", "application/json")])
        self.assertStatus(200)
        self.assertHeader('Content-Type', 'application/json')
        self.assertHeader('Allow', 'DELETE, GET, HEAD, POST, PUT')

    def test_03_REST_POST(self):
        blog = self.photoblog
        params = {'title': 'Test2',
                    'author': 'Test demo', 'description': 'blah blah',
                    'content': 'more blah blah bluh', 'blog_id':
                    str(blog.ID)}

        # let's transform the param dictionary
        # into a valid query string
        query_string = urllib.urlencode(params)

        self.getPage("/services/rest/album/", method="POST",
                    body=query_string,
                    headers=[("Accept", "application/json")])
        self.assertStatus(201)
        self.assertHeader('Content-Type', 'application/json')

        # here we miss the Accept header
        self.getPage("/services/rest/album/", method="POST",
                    body=query_string)
        self.assertStatus(406)

    def test_04_REST_PUT(self):
        blog = self.photoblog
        params = {'title': 'Test2',
                    'author': 'Test demo', 'description': 'blah blah',
                    'content': 'meh ehe eh', 'blog_id': str(blog.ID)}
        query_string = urllib.urlencode(params)

        # at this stage we don't have yet an album with that ID
        self.getPage("/services/rest/album/23", method="PUT",
                    body=query_string,
                    headers=[("Accept", "application/json")])
```

```python
        self.assertStatus(404)

        self.getPage("/services/rest/album/4", method="PUT",
                     body=query_string,
                     headers=[("Accept", "application/json")])
        self.assertStatus(200)
        self.assertHeader('Content-Type', 'application/json')

    def test_06_REST_DELETE(self):
        self.getPage("/services/rest/album/4", method="DELETE")
        self.assertStatus(200)

        # DELETE is idempotent and should always return 200 in case
        # of success
        self.getPage("/services/rest/album/4", method="DELETE")
        self.assertStatus(200)

    def test_05_REST_Collection_GET(self):
        self.getPage("/services/rest/albums/3")
        self.assertStatus(400, 'Invalid range')

        self.getPage("/services/rest/albums/a")
        self.assertStatus(400, 'Invalid range')

        self.getPage("/services/rest/albums/0-")
        self.assertStatus(400, 'Invalid range')

        self.getPage("/services/rest/albums/a+3")
        self.assertStatus(400, 'Invalid range')

        self.getPage("/services/rest/albums/3-a")
        self.assertStatus(400, 'Invalid range')

        self.getPage("/services/rest/albums/0+3")
        self.assertStatus(400, 'Invalid range')

        # valid range but missing Accept header
        self.getPage("/services/rest/albums/0-3")
        self.assertStatus(406)

        self.getPage("/services/rest/albums/0-3",
                     headers=[("Accept", "application/json")])
        self.assertStatus(200)
        self.assertHeader('Content-Type', 'application/json')
        json = simplejson.loads(self.body)
        self.failUnless(isinstance(json, list))
        self.failUnlessEqual(len(json), 3)
```

The test case above is only an example of different tests we can conduct against our application and in reality more tests would be required to ensure that the application works as expected and to perform regression testing.

As you can see, our test case performs HTTP requests and validates the content of the response as well as its headers. The simplicity of these validations is brought by the unit testing extension provided by the webtest module. Let's now see in detail how to set up that module to run the test case shown earlier.

First let's create a test.py module containing the following code:

```python
import os.path
import sys
# Tell Python where to find our application's modules.
sys.path.append(os.path.abspath('..'))

# CherryPy main test module
from cherrypy.test import test as cptest

# load the global application settings
current_dir = os.path.abspath(os.path.dirname(__file__))
conf.from_ini(os.path.join(current_dir, 'application.conf'))

from models import Photoblog, Album, Film, Photo

# dejavu main arena object
arena = storage.arena
# register our models with dejavu
storage.setup()

def initialize():

    for cls in (Photoblog, Album, Film, Photo):
        arena.create_storage(cls)

def shutdown():

    for cls in (Photoblog, Album, Film, Photo):
        if arena.has_storage(cls):
            arena.drop_storage(cls)

def run():
    """
    entry point to the test suite
    """
    try:
        initialize()
```

```
        # modules name without the trailing .py
        # that this test will run. They must belong
        # to the same directory as test.py
        test_list = ['test_models', 'test_services']
        cptest.CommandLineParser(test_list).run()
    finally:
        shutdown()
    print
    raw_input('hit enter to terminate the test')

if __name__ == '__main__':
    run()
```

Let's inspect what the `test.py` module can achieve:

```
sylvain@[test]$ python test.py --help

CherryPy Test Program
    Usage:
        test.py --server=* --host=127.0.0.1 --port=8080 --1.0 --cover
--basedir=path --profile --validate --conquer --dumb --tests**

    * servers:
        --server=modpygw: modpygw
        --server=wsgi: cherrypy._cpwsgi.CPWSGIServer (default)
        --server=cpmodpy: cpmodpy

    --host=<name or IP addr>: use a host other than the default
                             (127.0.0.1).
        Not yet available with mod_python servers.
    --port=<int>: use a port other than the default (8080)
    --1.0: use HTTP/1.0 servers instead of default HTTP/1.1
    --cover: turn on code-coverage tool
    --basedir=path: display coverage stats for some path other than
    --cherrypy.

    --profile: turn on profiling tool
    --validate: use wsgiref.validate (builtin in Python 2.5).
    --conquer: use wsgiconq (which uses pyconquer) to trace calls.
    --dumb: turn off the interactive output features.

    ** tests:
        --test_models
        --test_services
```

As you can see, our test supports a handful of functionalities allowing us to run our tests in different configurations such as by using the built-in HTTP server or a mod_python handler, as we will explain in Chapter 10.

Next we create a PhotoblogTest class, which will be the base class of our test cases. In a module called blogtest.py we add the following code:

```
from cherrypy.test import helper

# default blog name for the test suite
blog_name = u"photoblog"
from models import Photoblog

class PhotoblogTest(helper.CPWebCase):
    def photoblog(self):
        blog = Photoblog.find_by_name(blog_name)
        if not blog:
            self.fail("Could not find blog '%s'" % blog_name)

        return blog
    photoblog = property(photoblog, doc="Returns a blog object to
                         work against")
```

The PhotoblogTest class inherits from the CherryPy CPWebCase class, which provides a list of functions to perform assertions checking against a web test. For instance, the CPWebCase class defines the following:

- assertStatus(status) to verify the status of the last response
- assertHeader(name, value=None) to verify whether a header is present as well as ensure that the value, if not None, is the one provided
- assertBody(value) to check the returned body is the one we expected
- assertInBody(value) to verify the returned content contained a given value

This class also comes with the getPage(uri, method, headers, body) method to issue an HTTP request.

Our PhotoblogTest class defines the photoblog property so that tests can easily get a reference to the blog we create by default throughout the life of the test.

The blogtest.py module also contains the following functions used to set up the server for the life cycle of a test:

```
from lib import storage
import services
from models import Album, Film, Photo

def populate_storage():
```

```
    photoblog = Photoblog()
    photoblog.create(blog_name, u'Yeah')
    a1 = Album()
    a1.create(photoblog, "Test album",
                        "Test", "blah blah", "more blah blah")

def reset_storage():
    # here we simply remove every object a test has left
    # in the storage so that we have a clean
    # storage for the next test case run
    photoblog = Photoblog.find_by_name(blog_name)
    photoblog.delete()

def setup_photoblog_server():
    # Update the CherryPy global configuration
    cherrypy.config.update(os.path.join(current_dir, 'http.conf'))

    # fill the storage with default values for the purpose of the
    #test
    populate_storage()

    # Construct the published trees

    services_app = services.construct_app()

    # Mount the applications on the '/' prefix
    engine_conf_path = os.path.join(current_dir, 'engine.conf')

    service_app = cherrypy.tree.mount(services_app, '/services',
                                    config=engine_conf_path)
    service_app.merge(services.services_conf)

def teardown_photoblog_server():
    reset_storage()
```

The setup_photoblog_server() function is responsible for setting up the photoblog application and loading the different configuration settings. These must be a part of the test directory. For instance, we could provide a different database name for the storage to be used so that we do not run the test on a production database.

Finally, we define our test cases in a module named test_services.py as follows:

```
import httplib
import os.path
import urllib

import cherrypy
import simplejson

from models import Photoblog, Album, Film, Photo
```

```
from blogtest import PhotoblogTest, blog_name, \
    setup_photoblog_server, teardown_photoblog_server

current_dir = os.path.abspath(os.path.dirname(__file__))

def setup_server():
    setup_photoblog_server()

def teardown_server():
    teardown_photoblog_server()

# Here we insert the TestServicesREST class definition
# that we have seen at the beginning of this section
```

Let's explain how this module is constructed:

1. We must import a bunch of modules to perform specific tasks for our tests.

2. Our test case subclasses the `PhotoblogTest` class that we have described earlier.

3. We need to define two functions — `setup_server()` and `teardown_server()`, which will be automatically called by the CherryPy test module each time it starts and finishes running a test module. This allows us to initialize our photoblog application for the test case.

4. Finally we add the `TestServicesREST` class as our test case.

Let's now run the entire test suite:

```
sylvain@[test]$ python test.py
Python version used to run this test script: 2.5
CherryPy version 3.0.0
HTTP server version HTTP/1.1

Running tests: cherrypy._cpwsgi.CPWSGIServer
No handlers could be found for logger "cherrypy.error"
test_00_Photoblog_unit (test_models.TestModels) ... ok
test_01_Photoblog_create (test_models.TestModels) ... ok
test_02_Photoblog_retrieve_by_name (test_models.TestModels) ... ok
test_03_Photoblog_retrieve_by_unknown_name (test_models.TestModels)
                                                    ... ok
test_04_Photoblog_retrieve_by_unsupported_id_type
  (test_models.TestModels) ... ok
test_05_Photoblog_update (test_models.TestModels) ... ok
test_06_Photoblog_populate (test_models.TestModels) ... ok
test_10_Album_unit (test_models.TestModels) ... ok
test_99_Photoblog_delete (test_models.TestModels) ... ok
test_00_REST (test_services.TestServicesREST) ... ok
```

```
test_01_REST_HEAD (test_services.TestServicesREST) ... ok
test_02_REST_GET (test_services.TestServicesREST) ... ok
test_03_REST_POST (test_services.TestServicesREST) ... ok
test_04_REST_PUT (test_services.TestServicesREST) ... ok
test_05_REST_Collection_GET (test_services.TestServicesREST) ... ok
test_06_REST_DELETE (test_services.TestServicesREST) ... ok
```

If on the other hand you wish to run only one module:

```
sylvain@[test]$ python test.py --models
Python version used to run this test script: 2.5
CherryPy version 3.0.0
HTTP server version HTTP/1.1

Running tests: cherrypy._cpwsgi.CPWSGIServer
No handlers could be found for logger "cherrypy.error"
test_00_Photoblog_unit (test_models.TestModels) ... ok
test_01_Photoblog_create (test_models.TestModels) ... ok
test_02_Photoblog_retrieve_by_name (test_models.TestModels) ... ok
test_03_Photoblog_retrieve_by_unknown_name (test_models.TestModels)
                                                         ... ok
test_04_Photoblog_retrieve_by_unsupported_id_type (test_models.
                                              TestModels) ... ok
test_05_Photoblog_update (test_models.TestModels) ... ok
test_06_Photoblog_populate (test_models.TestModels) ... ok
test_10_Album_unit (test_models.TestModels) ... ok
test_99_Photoblog_delete (test_models.TestModels) ... ok
```

As you can see, writing unit tests using the CherryPy test module makes the task of testing an application based on CherryPy an easy one, because CherryPy takes care of a lot of common burdens allowing the tester to focus on what really matters.

Performance and Load Testing

Depending on the application you are writing and your expectations in terms of volume, you may need to run load and performance testing in order to detect potential bottlenecks in the application that are preventing it from reaching a certain level of performance.

This section will not detail how to conduct a performance or load test as it is out of its scope but we will review one Python solution, the FunkLoad package provided by Nuxeo, a French company specialized in free software written in Python. You can install FunkLoad via the `easy_install` command. FunkLoad is available at `http://funkload.nuxeo.org/`.

FunkLoad is an extension to the `webunit` module, a Python module oriented towards unit testing web application. FunkLoad comes with a fairly extensive API and set of tools taking care of the burden of extracting metrics from a load test to eventually generate test reports with nice-looking charts.

Let's see an extremely basic example of using FunkLoad.

```
from funkload.FunkLoadTestCase import FunkLoadTestCase

class LoadHomePage(FunkLoadTestCase):
    def test_homepage(self):
        server_url = self.conf_get('main', 'url')
        nb_time = self.conf_getInt('test_homepage', 'nb_time')

        home_page = "%s/" % server_url
        for i in range(nb_time):
            self.logd('Try %i' % i)
            self.get(home_page, description='Get gome page')

if __name__ in ('main', '__main__'):
    import unittest
    unittest.main()
```

Let's understand this example in detail:

1. Your test case must inherit from the `FunkLoadTestCase` class so that FunkLoad can do its internal job of tracking what happens during the test.

2. Your class name is important as FunkLoad will look for a file named after that name, in our case: `LoadHomePage.conf` in the test directory.

3. Your test has direct access to the configuration file and gets values as follows:
   - `conf_get(section, key)` returns a string.
   - `conf_getInt(section, key)` returns the value as an integer.
   - `conf_getFloat(section key)` returns the value as a float.
   - `conf_getList(section, key)` returns the value column separated as a list of strings.

4. You then simply call the `get()` or `post()` method to issue a request against the server and retrieve the response returned by these methods.

Internally Funkload will create a set of metrics of the test and save them in an XML file that can be processed later.

Let's analyze the `LoadHomePage.conf` settings:

```
[main]
title=Photoblog home page
description=Access the photoblog home page
url=http://localhost:8080

[test_homepage]
description=Access %(nb_time)s times the following pages:
 %(pages)s.
nb_time=3
pages=/

[ftest]
log_to = console file
log_path = logs/load_home_page.log
result_path = logs/load_home_page.xml
sleep_time_min = 0
sleep_time_max = 2
```

The `main` section contains global settings for the test, whereas the `test_homepage` contains specific values for the `test_homepage()` method of our test case. The `ftest` section is used by FunkLoad for internal processing.

After starting an instance of the photoblog application server, we run the test:

```
sylvain@[test]$ python test_load_home_page.py
test_homepage: Starting ------------------------------------
        Access 3 times the following pages: /.
test_homepage: Try 0
test_homepage: GET: http://localhost:8080/
        Page 1: Get gome page ...
test_homepage:   Done in 0.039s
test_homepage:   Load css and images...
test_homepage:    Done in 0.044s
test_homepage: Try 1
test_homepage: GET: http://localhost:8080/
        Page 2: Get gome page ...
test_homepage:   Done in 0.041s
test_homepage:   Load css and images...
test_homepage:    Done in 0.000s
test_homepage: Try 2
test_homepage: GET: http://localhost:8080/
        Page 3: Get gome page ...
test_homepage:   Done in 0.051s
test_homepage:   Load css and images...
test_homepage:    Done in 0.000s
```

```
                  .
     ------------------------------------------------------------------
     Ran 1 test in 2.149s

     OK
```

The previous test is not really a load test yet. To use it as a load or performance test, we need to use a FunkLoad tool called `fl-run-bench`. This command-line tool will run a benchmark using a test like the one we have just created.

A benchmark will simulate virtual users to run concurrently to perform a realistic use of the server. For instance, if we want to benchmark three cycles of 5, 10, and 20 virtual users during 30 seconds, we would do the following.

First add the following sections to the configuration file:

```
[bench]
cycles = 5:10:20
duration = 30
startup_delay = 0.05
sleep_time = 1
cycle_time = 1
log_to = file
log_path = logs/load_home_page.log
result_path = logs/load_home_page.xml
sleep_time_min = 0
sleep_time_max = 0.6
```

Then launch the benchmark:

```
sylvain@[test]$ fl-run-bench test_load_home_page.py \
  LoadHomePage.test_homepage

========================================
Benching LoadHomePage.test_homepage
========================================
Access 3 times the following pages: /.
------------------------------------------------------------------
- - -

Configuration
=============

* Current time: 2007-02-28T13:43:22.376339
* Configuration file: load/LoadHomePage.conf
* Log xml: logs/load_home_page.xml
* Server: http://localhost:8080
* Cycles: [5, 10, 20]
```

```
* Cycle duration: 30s
* Sleeptime between request: from 0.0s to 0.6s
* Sleeptime between test case: 1.0s
* Startup delay between thread: 0.05s

Benching
========

Cycle #0 with 5 virtual users
-----------------------------

* Current time: 2007-02-28T13:43:22.380481
* Starting threads: ..... done.
* Logging for 30s (until 2007-02-28T13:43:52.669762): .... done.
* Waiting end of threads: ..... done.
* Waiting cycle sleeptime 1s: ... done.
* End of cycle, 33.46s elapsed.
* Cycle result: **SUCCESSFUL**, 76 success, 0 failure, 0 errors.

Cycle #1 with 10 virtual users
------------------------------

* Current time: 2007-02-28T13:43:55.837831
* Starting threads: .... done.
* Logging for 30s (until 2007-02-28T13:44:26.681356): .... done.
* Waiting end of threads: ......... done.
* Waiting cycle sleeptime 1s: ... done.
* End of cycle, 34.02s elapsed.
* Cycle result: **SUCCESSFUL**, 145 success, 0 failure, 0 errors.

Cycle #2 with 20 virtual users
------------------------------

* Current time: 2007-02-28T13:44:29.859868
* Starting threads: ....... done.
* Logging for 30s (until 2007-02-28T13:45:01.191106):
* Waiting end of threads: .................. done.
* Waiting cycle sleeptime 1s: ... done.
* End of cycle, 35.59s elapsed.
* Cycle result: **SUCCESSFUL**, 203 success, 0 failure, 0 errors.

Result
======

* Success: 424
* Failures: 0
* Errors: 0

Bench status: **SUCCESSFUL**
```

Now that we have run our benchmark we can create a report using the
fl-build-report command-line tool as follows:

```
sylvain@[test]$ fl-build-report --html -o reports
 logs/load_home_page.xml
Creating html report: ...done:
reports/test_homepage-2007-02-28T13-43-22/index.html
```

This will produce an HTML page with statistics gathered from the benchmark as shown in the following figure:

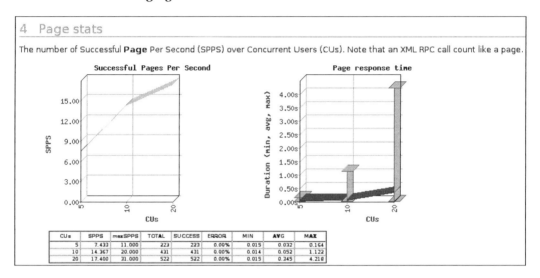

In addition to these modules, FunkLoad offers tools to test XML-RPC servers or record tests from a browser directly, allowing for complex tests to be developed easily. Kindly refer the FunkLoad documentation for more details about these features.

Overall Funkload is quite a powerful tool and yet flexible and simple to use, providing a comprehensive load and performance-testing environment for Python web applications.

Functional Testing

Once your application functionalities start taking shape, you may want to conduct a set of functional testing so that you can validate your application's correctness regarding the specification. For a web application, this would mean going through the application from a browser for example. However, since the test would have to be automated it would require the use of third-party products such as Selenium (Selenium is available at http://www.openqa.org/selenium/).

Selenium is a JavaScript-based open-source product, developed and maintained by the OpenQA team to perform functional and acceptance testing. It works directly from the browser it targets helping to ensure the portability of the client-side code of the application.

Selenium comes in several packages:

- Core: The core package allows a tester to design and run tests directly from the browser using pure HTML and JavaScript.

- Remote Control: This package allows performing tests using common programming languages such as Python, Perl, Ruby, Java, or C#. Scripts written in these languages drive a browser to automate actions to be performed during the test.

- IDE: The Selenium IDE is available as a Firefox extension to help the creation of tests by recording actions carried out via the browser itself. The tests can then be exported to be used by the Core and Remote Control packages.

Application under Test

Before we explain how Selenium components work, we must introduce an application example. This application will simply provide one web page with two links. One of them will replace the current page with a new one. The second link will fetch data using Ajax. We use this example rather than our photoblog application for the sake of simplicity. The code of the application is as follows:

```python
import datetime
import os.path

import cherrypy
import simplejson

_header = """<html>
<head><title>Selenium test</title></head>
<script type="application/javascript" src="MochiKit/MochiKit.js">
</script>
<script type="application/javascript" src="MochiKit/New.js">
</script>
<script type="application/javascript">
var fetchReport = function() {
    var xmlHttpReq = getXMLHttpRequest();
    xmlHttpReq.open("GET", "/fetch_report", true);

    xmlHttpReq.setRequestHeader('Accept', 'application/json');
    var d = sendXMLHttpRequest(xmlHttpReq);
```

```
        d.addCallback(function (data) {
            var reportData = evalJSONRequest(data);
            swapDOM($('reportName'), SPAN({'id': 'reportName'},
                    reportData['name']));
            swapDOM($('reportAuthor'), SPAN({'id': 'reportAuthor'},
                    reportData['author']));
            swapDOM($('reportUpdated'), SPAN({'id': 'reportUpdated'},
                    reportData['updated']));
        });
}
</script>
<body>
<div>
<a href="javascript:void(0);" onclick="fetchReport();">Get report via
 Ajax</a>
<br />
<a href="report">Get report</a>
</div>
<br />
"""


_footer = """
</body>
</html>
"""


class Dummy:
    @cherrypy.expose
    def index(self):
        return """%s
<div id="report">
  <span>Name:</span>
  <span id="reportName"></span>
  <br />
  <span>Author:</span>
  <span id="reportAuthor"></span>
  <br />
  <span>Updated:</span>
  <span id="reportUpdated"></span>
</div>%s""" % (_header, _footer)
```

```python
    @cherrypy.expose
    def report(self):
        now = datetime.datetime.now().strftime("%d %b. %Y, %H:%M:%S")
        return """%s
<div id="report">
  <span>Name:</span>
  <span id="reportName">Music report (HTML)</span>
  <br />
  <span>Author:</span>
  <span id="reportAuthor">Jon Doe</span>
  <br />
  <span>Updated:</span>
  <span id="reportUpdated">%s</span>
</div>%s""" % (_header, now, _footer)

    @cherrypy.expose
    def fetch_report(self):
        now = datetime.datetime.now().strftime("%d %b. %Y, %H:%M:%S")
        cherrypy.response.headers['Content-Type'] =
         'application/json'
        return simplejson.dumps({'name': 'Music report (Ajax)',
                                 'author': 'Jon Doe',
                                 'updated': now})

if __name__ == '__main__':
    current_dir = os.path.abspath(os.path.dirname(__file__))
    conf = {'/test': {'tools.staticdir.on': True,
                      'tools.staticdir.dir': "test",
                      'tools.staticdir.root': current_dir},
            '/MochiKit': {'tools.staticdir.on': True,
                          'tools.staticdir.dir': "MochiKit",
                          'tools.staticdir.root': current_dir},
            '/selenium': {'tools.staticdir.on': True,
                          'tools.staticdir.dir': "selenium",
                          'tools.staticdir.root': current_dir}}
    cherrypy.quickstart(Dummy(), config=conf)
```

We define three paths to be served as static directories. The first one carries our
Selenium test suite and test cases that will be detailed later. The second one
contains the MochiKit JavaScript toolkit and the last one contains the Selenium Core
package. Indeed, Selenium Core must be served by the same server under which the
tests are conducted.

The application will look like the following in the browser:

```
Get report via Ajax
Get report

Name:
Author:
Updated:
```

When clicking on the first link, the `fetch_report()` JavaScript function will be triggered to fetch the report data via `XMLHttpRequest`. The result will look like the following:

```
Get report via Ajax
Get report

Name: Music report (Ajax)
Author: Jon Doe
Updated: 28 Feb. 2007, 15:03:45
```

When clicking on the second link, the current page will be replaced by a new page containing the report such as the following:

```
Get report via Ajax
Get report

Name: Music report (HTML)
Author: Jon Doe
Updated: 28 Feb. 2007, 15:04:04
```

As you can see this application is not doing anything fancy but provides us with common use cases in modern web applications. In the following sections we will therefore describe two test cases, one for each link of our application.

Selenium Core

Selenium tests are described via HTML tables of three columns and as many rows as needed with each row describing an action to be performed by Selenium. The three columns are as follows:

- Name of the Selenium action to be performed.
- Target to be looked for by Selenium within the document object model of the page. It can be the identifier of an element or an XPath statement leading to an element.
- Value. A value to compare to or to be used by the action.

Let's describe for example the following test:

1. Fetch the home page.
2. Click on the **Get Report** link and wait for the returned page.
3. Verify that we can find the HTML string in the new page.

This would translate into (save this in `test/test_html.html`):

```
<html>
<head />
<body>
<table>
<thead>
<tr><td rowspan="1" colspan="3">HTML Test</td></tr>
</thead>
<tbody>
<tr>
    <td>open</td>
    <td>/</td>
    <td></td>
</tr>
<tr>
    <td>clickAndWait</td>
    <td>link=Get report</td>
    <td></td>
</tr>
<tr>
    <td>verifyTextPresent</td>
    <td></td>
    <td>HTML</td>
</tr>
</tbody>
</table>
</body>
</html>
```

Let's describe now our second use case to test our Ajax code:

1. Fetch the home page.
2. Click on the **Get Report via Ajax** link.
3. Pause for a few seconds.
4. Verify that we can find the Ajax string in the new page.

The third step is compulsory because when performing an XMLHttpRequest, Selenium does not wait for the response. In such a case, you must pause Selenium's execution so that it gives time for the response to come back and update the document object model of the page. The previous use case will translate into (save this in test/test_ajax.html):

```
<html>
<head />
<body>
<table cellpadding="1" cellspacing="1" border="1">
<thead>
<tr><td rowspan="1" colspan="3">Test Ajax</td></tr>
</thead>
<tbody>
<tr>
    <td>open</td>
    <td>/</td>
    <td></td>
</tr>
<tr>
    <td>click</td>
    <td>link=Get report via Ajax</td>
    <td></td>
</tr>
<tr>
    <td>pause</td>
    <td>300</td>
    <td></td>
</tr>
<tr>
    <td>verifyTextPresent</td>
    <td></td>
    <td>Ajax</td>
</tr>
</tbody>
</table>
</body>
</html>
```

Now that we have our test cases in our test directory, we can create a test suite as follows:

```
<html>
<head>
<link rel="stylesheet" type="text/css"
 href="/selenium/core/selenium.css" />
<head>
```

```
<body>
 <table class="selenium">
  <tbody>
    <tr><td><b>Test Suite</b></td></tr>
    <tr><td><a href="test_html.html">Test HTML</a></td></tr>
    <tr><td><a href="test_ajax.html">Test Ajax</a></td></tr>
  </tbody>
 </table>
</body>
</html>
```

We now have everything we need to run a test. To do so, we will use the test runner provided by the Selenium Core package. In a browser open the following page:

```
http://localhost:8080/selenium/core/TestRunner.html
```

This will display a page like the following:

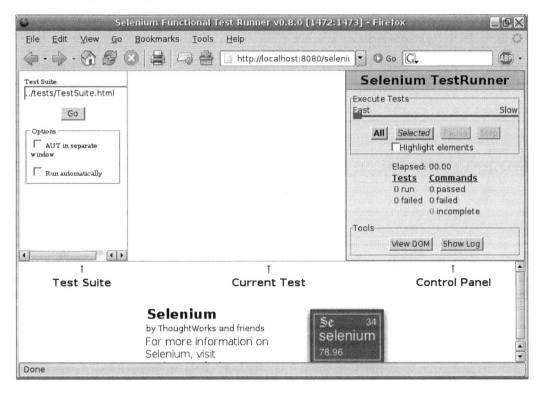

We can now load our test suite and get the next screen by entering the following path: `../../test/testsuite.html` in the **TestSuite** input box on the top left of the page.

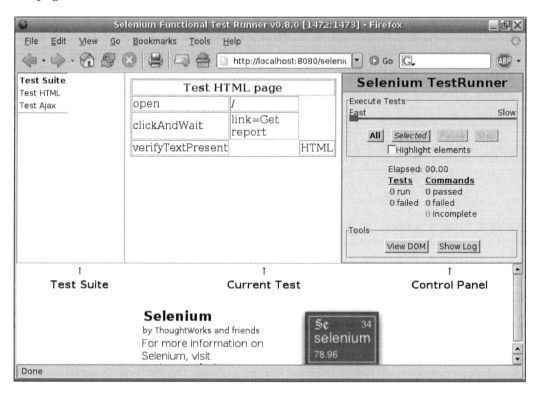

As you can see, the left pane lists all our test cases, the central pane displays the current selected test case, and the right pane shows Selenium's controls and results. Finally, the bottom of the page will display the result web page of each test case.

The next step is to run these tests by clicking the **All** button, which will generate the following screen:

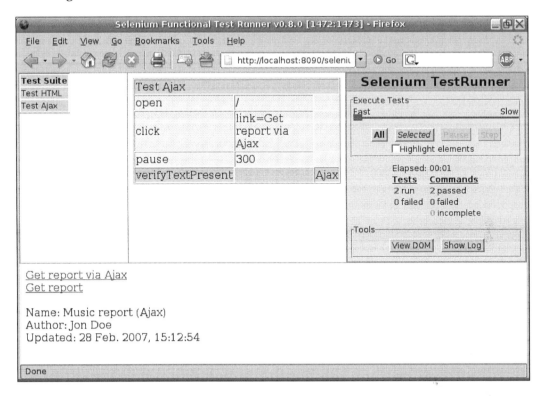

Selenium TestRunner will use color codes to inform you of how test cases have performed. Green means things were fine, yellow means the step is not finished, and red shows errors during the test.

Selenium IDE

In the previous section we have written our test cases directly from a text editor, which can become a little tedious with long use cases. Thankfully, the OpenQA team provides an integrated development editor for Selenium available as an extension for the Mozilla Firefox browser. The advantages of this IDE are:

- No need to install Selenium core package on the server
- Ability to record actions by following the business process in the browser
- Ability to manually amend any generated test
- Step-by-step debugging of test cases
- Recorded test cases can be exported to HTML or any of the supported languages of the Selenium Remote Control package

To record a test case you first need to provide the base URL of your server, `http://localhost:8080` in the following window:

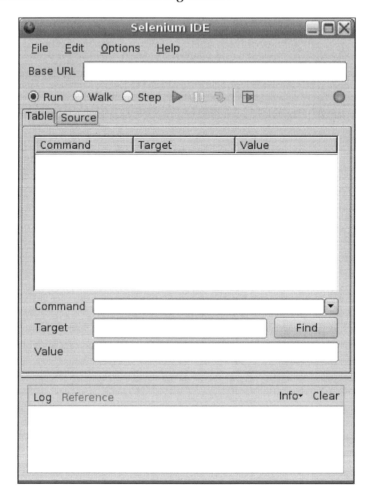

Since by default when you start the IDE it runs in recording mode, you can now go to the browser and follow your business process. Each step will be recorded automatically by the Selenium IDE. For instance, by clicking on **Get Report**, the **clickAndWait** step will be generated. To verify the presence of a given text, you must highlight the targeted text, right-click to open the pop-up menu, and select **verifyTextPresent**.

Your IDE will then look like the following:

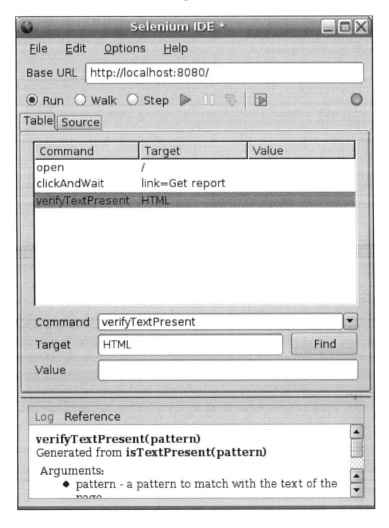

Now that we have a recorded test we can run it by clicking the green triangle.

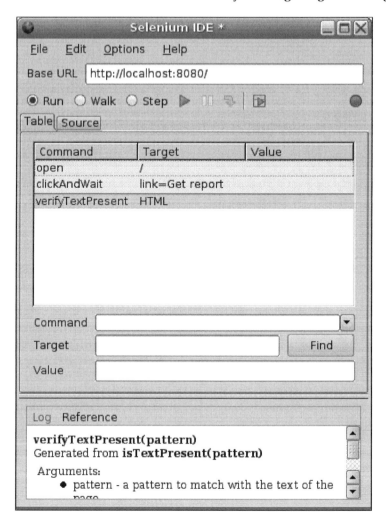

As you can see, the steps to create a script are much simpler using the IDE. Moreover, thanks to its great flexibility you can either insert new steps or remove and modify existing ones if the IDE failed to record an action for instance. You can also load tests created manually into the IDE and run them from there.

Finally, you can export your recorded step so that you can run it via the Test Runner or via the Selenium Remote Control package as we will see in the next section.

Selenium Remote Control

The Selenium **Remote Control (RC)** package offers the possibility of driving a browser using a recorded step from several programming languages. This is extremely interesting because your tests can therefore be run as regular unit tests.

You need to first get the Python modules from the Selenium RC package. Once they can be found in your PYTHONPATH, you should be able to do the following: from selenium import selenium.

Next step will be to export the previously recorded test to the Python language. The resulting script will look like the following:

```python
from selenium import selenium
import unittest, time, re

class TestHTML(unittest.TestCase):
    def setUp(self):
        self.verificationErrors = []
        self.selenium = selenium("localhost", 4444, "*firefox",
                                 "http://localhost:8080")
        self.selenium.start()

    def test_TestHTML(self):
        # Get a reference to our selenium object
        sl = self.selenium

        sl.open("/")
        sl.click("link=Get report")
        sl.wait_for_page_to_load("5000")
        try: self.failUnless(sl.is_text_present("HTML"))
        except AssertionError, e: self.verificationErrors.append(str(e))

    def tearDown(self):
        self.selenium.stop()
        self.assertEqual([], self.verificationErrors)

if __name__ == "__main__":
    unittest.main()
```

As you can see, this is a pure test case from the unittest standard module.

Let's see what the script does:

1. The `setUp()` method, called before each test method, initializes a Selenium object indicating the host and the port of the Selenium proxy as well as which kind of browser should be used during the test.

2. The `test_TestHTML()` method performs the actual steps of our test case.

3. The `tearDown()` method, called after each test method, stops this instance of the Selenium object.

Before running the test, you must start the Selenium proxy, which will handle the startup of the chosen browser as well as run the test. It will then return all the results to our test case.

The Selenium RC package comes with a default proxy server written in Java, which is the one we will use in our example. However, nothing prevents anyone from writing a proxy in a different language of course. To start the server, you must go to the Selenium RC package directory and issue the following command, assuming you have a Java virtual machine 1.4.2 or above installed on your machine:

```
sylvain@[selenium]$ java -jar server/selenium-server.jar
```

Once the server is started, you must start your application server and then you can run the test as follows:

```
python test_html.py
.
----------------------------------------------------------------
Ran 1 test in 6.877s

OK
```

If you look at the Selenium proxy server logs, you should see something like the following:

```
queryString =
cmd=getNewBrowserSession&1=%2Afirefox&2=http%3A%2F%2Flocalhost%3A8080
Preparing Firefox profile...
Launching Firefox...
3 oct. 2006 17:35:10 org.mortbay.util.Container start
INFO: Started HttpContext[/,/]
Got result: OK,1159893304958
queryString = cmd=open&1=%2F&sessionId=1159893304958
Got result: OK
queryString = cmd=click&1=link%3DGet+report&sessionId=1159893304958
Got result: OK
queryString = cmd=waitForPageToLoad&1=5000&sessionId=1159893304958
Got result: OK
```

```
queryString = cmd=isTextPresent&1=HTML&sessionId=1159893304958
Got result: OK,true
queryString = cmd=testComplete&sessionId=1159893304958
Killing Firefox...
Got result: OK
```

This will launch a Firefox instance, run the test, and pass back the results to your test case as normal input.

In this section, we have presented an open-source solution, Selenium, to perform acceptance and functional testing in order to validate the correctness of our application. Although this solution is not the only one, it has gained lots of support from the community. Its flexibility and large set of features offer the tester a large palette to build his or her tests on.

Summary

Throughout this chapter we have presented different aspects of testing an application. Although this is not a comprehensive list of what can be achieved, it should provide a good starting point to understand how an application can and should be tested. It is important to note that testing should not happen at the last stage of the application development's life but instead be a part of its building as soon as possible.

10
Deployment

Our final chapter will explain in the first section how to configure CherryPy-based applications, and then review different methods to deploy such an application through the use of Apache and lighttpd. Finally, we will review how to make your CherryPy-based application SSL enabled via the built-in CherryPy HTTP server, as well as by using Apache and lighttpd capabilities.

Configuration

While developing an application, you always need to parameterize it, so that it can be tuned as per the requirements of the hosting environment. For instance, the type of database used, PostgreSQL or MySQL, the directory in which the application resides, administrator contacts, etc.

There are different levels of configuration settings required in a web application like our photoblog:

- Web server: Settings linked to the HTTP server
- Engine: Settings associated with the engine hosting the application
- Application: Settings our application will use

CherryPy—Web and Engine Configuration System

Since our application is using CherryPy, we will use the CherryPy configuration capabilities for the web server and the engine. CherryPy uses a configuration based on the syntax of the INI format defined by Microsoft.

The format of a CherryPy configuration file is as follows:

```
[section]
key = value
```

The main difference between the original INI format and the format used by CherryPy is the fact that values in the latter case are Python data types. For example:

```
[global]
server.socket_host = "localhost"
server.socket_port = 8080
```

With the exception of `[global]`, the sections of configuration files match a requested URI path segment, as illustrated in the following example:

```
[/css/style.css]
tools.staticfile.on = True
tools.staticfile.file = "app.css"
tools.staticfile.root = "/var/www/photoblog/design/default/css"
```

When CherryPy tries to match the `/css/style.css` request, it will inspect the configuration settings for a matching section. If found, it will use the settings defined for that section.

Before we explain how CherryPy differentiates between the web server and the engine settings, let's see how the configuration settings can be defined in a Python dictionary instead. The following code snippet demonstrates the same settings:

```
{'/css/style.css': {'tools.staticfile.on': True,
    'tools.staticfilE.file': "app.css" 'tools.staticfile.root':
    "/var/www/photoblog/design/default/css"}}
```

Functionally, both methods will provide the same capabilities. Using a Python dictionary offers the advantage of residing within the code itself, and thus allows for more complex data types to be provided as values. Eventually, it is usually a matter of taste between the two options.

Now that we have presented how to declare configuration settings, let's see how to pass them to their components. CherryPy API is quite straight forward in that respect:

- `cherrypy.config.update` (file or dictionary) is used to configure the CherryPy web server.
- `cherrypy.tree.mount` (app, config file, or dictionary) is used to provide the settings for the mounted application.

- The _cp_config attribute is bound to the page handlers, or to the class containing the page handlers and calls a controller defined as a dictionary (in which case, the settings are propagated by CherryPy to all the page handlers of that controller). It is used to pass the settings directly to where they will be needed.

We will review an example to understand how to use that API in our context:

```python
import cherrypy
class Root:
  @cherrypy.expose
  def echo(self, some):
    repeat = cherrypy.request.config.get('repeat', 1)
    return some * repeat
  echo._cp_config = {'repeat': 3}

if __name__ == '__main__':
  http_conf = {'global': {'environment': 'production',
                          'server.socket_port': 9090,
                          'log.screen': True,
                          'log.error_file': 'error.log',
                          'log.access_file': 'access.log'}}
  cherrypy.config.update(http_conf)

  app0_conf = {'/echo': {'tools.response_headers.on': True,
                         'tools.response_headers.headers':
                         ('Content-Type', 'text/plain')]}}
  cherrypy.tree.mount(Root(), script_name='/app0',
                                config=app0_conf)

  app1_conf = {'/echo': {'tools.gzip.on': True,
                         'repeat': 2}}
  cherrypy.tree.mount(Root(), script_name='/app1',
                                config=app1_conf)

  cherrypy.server.quickstart()
  cherrypy.engine.start()
```

Let's see what we have done in our example:

1. First we declare an application with a page handler named echo. The purpose of this handler is to return the request body and repeat it as many times as defined by the configuration setting key repeat. To do so, we use the _cp_config attribute bound to the page handler. This value can also be passed from the main configuration dictionary. In that case, the value coming from the main dictionary takes precedence over the _cp_config attribute.

2. Next we declare the web server settings in a dictionary and then we call `cherrypy.config.update()` with that dictionary. Note that the use of the key, named global, is not compulsory when using a dictionary. CherryPy does interpret it exactly the same way; so the semantic equivalent of the previous example can be written as follows:

```
http_conf = {'environment': 'production',
             'server.socket_port': 9090,
             'log.screen': True,
             'log.error_file': 'error.log',
             'log.access_file': 'access.log'}
cherrypy.config.update(http_conf)
```

3. Finally we mount two applications on two distinct prefixes with two different configuration settings. It is important to notice that the key we use is the path to the page handler relatively to where the application is mounted. That is why we use /echo, and neither /app0/echo nor /app1/echo. This also means that configuration settings do not leak across mounted applications. CherryPy makes sure that each application receives only the settings it was declared with.

 It is a common mistake to pass configuration settings associated with the application to the `cherrypy.config.update()` method. This will not propagate the settings to the mounted application. You must use the `config` attribute of `cherrypy.tree.mount()` to get the expected behavior.

Photoblog Application Configuration System

Configuration settings of an application will not usually be passed through the CherryPy configuration system, which is at a lower level. An application would usually define entities from their domain level, store those values in a back-end storage along with the rest of its data, and ultimately provide a front-end interface to allow the administrator or a user to modify them.

The photoblog application will not go that far but will keep a fairly simple approach to providing configuration settings by using a pure INI file. We make this choice because in the photoblog application case the configuration settings will be simple, defined, and editable by the administrator of the application. We will therefore avoid the burden of developing a more complex solution than an INI file.

However, in order to simplify access to those settings, we will define a specific class that will turn the INI sections, keys, and values into a Python object:

```
from ConfigParser import ConfigParser

class Config(object):

  def from_ini(self, filepath, encoding='ISO-8859-1'):
    config = ConfigParser()
    config.readfp(file(filepath, 'rb'))

    for section in config.sections():
      section_prop = Config()
      section_prop.keys = []
      setattr(self, section, section_prop)
      for option in config.options(section):
        section_prop.keys.append(option)
        value = config.get(section, option).decode(encoding)
        setattr(section_prop, option, value)
```

This class will simply go through the INI file and add attributes to the instance of the `Config` class on the fly. For instance, imagine you have the following INI file:

```
[app]
base_url = http://localhost:8080
copyright = Creative Commons Attribution-ShareAlike2.5 License

[storage]
host = localhost
dbname = photoblog
user = test
password = test
type = postgres
```

Using the above class, we can make the following modifications:

```
import config
c = config.Config()
c.from_ini('application.conf')

dir(c)
  ['__class__', '__delattr__', '__dict__', '__doc__',
   '__getattribute__', '__hash__', '__init__', '__module__'
   '__new__', '__reduce__', '__reduce_ex__', '__repr__',
   '__setattr__', '__str__', '__weakref__', 'app', 'storage']

c.app.copyright
u'Creative Commons Attribution-ShareAlike2.5 License'
```

As you can see, we have now modified the INI file into a tree of attributes bound to the instance of the `Config` class. The photoblog application will have one global instance of that class that will therefore be accessible from everywhere in the application.

In this section, we have briefly reviewed the ways to parameterize a CherryPy application using its built-in configuration system. We have also introduced a simple configuration system using an INI file format allowing application settings. This approach hence provides an easy way to mock up the passing of parameters, before moving towards a system-based database, which can be more demanding.

Deployment

Deploying a CherryPy-based application can be as easy as dropping the application in an environment, where all the required packages (CherryPy, Kid, simplejson, etc.) are available from the Python system path. However, in a shared web-hosted environment, it is quite likely that the CherryPy web server will reside behind a front-end server such as Apache or lighttpd, allowing the host provider to perform some filtering operations if needed, or for instance let that front end serve the static files in a more efficient fashion than CherryPy.

This section will present a few solutions to run a CherryPy application behind the Apache and lighttpd web servers.

Before explaining how to use CherryPy behind Apache or lighttpd, let's define a simple application that we will use throughout the example:

```
import.cherrypy
def setup_app():
  class Root:
    @cherrypy.expose
    def index(self):
      # Will return the hostname used by CherryPy and the remote
      # caller IP address
      return "Hello there %s from IP: %s " %
        (cherrypy.request.base, cherrypy.request.remote.ip)

  cherrypy.config.update({'server.socket_port': 9091,
                          'environment': 'production',
                          'log.screen': False,
                          'show_tracebacks': False})
  cherrypy.tree.mount(Root())

if __name__ == '__main__':
  setup_app()
  cherrypy.server.quickstart()
  cherrypy.engine.start()
```

As discussed earlier, there are several ways of deploying CherryPy-based applications. Now, we will discuss the different approaches to deployment.

Apache with mod_rewrite Module

The first solution you can review when running behind the Apache web server is to use the mod_rewrite module. This module allows you to define a set of rules that the module will analyze to transform incoming HTTP requests and re-dispatch them towards the back-end server.

In our example, we will make the following assumptions, which are in fact the requirements:

- You run Apache 2.2.

- You have access to the Apache configuration that can usually be found in the file named httpd.conf. You can also stop and restart the apache process. These requirements imply either that you have administrator rights on the machine or that you have a local installation of Apache to play with.

- You will use the VirtualHost directive that allows encapsulating directives targeting only one particular host. This allows distinct hosts to be handled by one single instance of Apache.

- We will also assume that you have myapp.com resolvable locally. To do so:

  Under Linux, add the following line to the /etc/hosts file:

  ```
  127.0.0.1 myapp.com myapp www.myapp.com
  ```

  Your operating system should now resolve requests to the myapp.com host to your local environment.

Let's now explain how we must configure Apache:

1. Load the required Apache modules, as follows:

   ```
   LoadModule rewrite_module modules/mod_rewrite.so
   ```

   Note that you may need to provide the full path to the module itself in some environments.

2. Next we declare the VirtualHost, as follows:

   ```
   # Create a virtual host in your apache configuration
   # to handle requests for the myapp.com hostname
   <VirtualHost 127.0.0.1:80>
     ServerName myapp.com
     ServerAlias www.myapp.com
     # Where our application files reside
   ```

```
DocumentRoot /home/sylvain/photoblog
# What is our directory index by default
DirectoryIndex index.html
# Message to return when our CherryPy server is down and
# apache could not forward the request.
ErrorDocument 502 "Server down"
# mod_proxy magic
# First enable the mod_rewrite engine
RewriteEngine on
# Now we simply rewrite incoming requests URI so that they
# are proxied to our CherryPy web server
# http://myapp.com/archives/2006/10/12/my-article
#    would become
# http://127.0.0.1:9091/archives/2006/10/12/my-article
RewriteRule ^(.*) http://127.0.0.1:9091$1 [P]

# Now define the format of the logs to be used by Apache
LogFormat "%h %l %u %t \"%r\" %>s %b \"%{Referer}i\"
  \"%{User-Agent}i\"" combined LogFormat
  "%t %a %D %I %O %s %{Content-Type}o %{Host}i
  \"%r\" \"%{Referer}i\"" host
CustomLog /home/sylvain/photoblog/access_myapp.log combined
  Errorlog /home/sylvain/photoblog/error_myapp.log
</VirtualHost>
```

3. The next step is to stop and restart your Apache process so that these modifications are taken into account.

4. Then start your CherryPy application server.

The `mod_rewrite` module documentation explains in detail how to build rewriting rules. In the previous example, we defined the most generic one by mapping the request URI path to a new hostname.

When navigating to the URL `http://myapp.com`, you should now see the following message:

```
Hello there http://127.0.0.1:9091 from IP: 127.0.0.1
```

Now that we know how to map a host to our CherryPy application via Apache, we might want to retrieve the actual hostname and remote IP address instead of the local ones. The former is needed when generating links like:

```
link = "%s/%s" % (cherrypy.request.base, path)
```

There are two options to achieve this, as they are independent from each other:

1. Use the `mod_proxy` module of Apache to forward the host.
   - First you need to load the module like this (consult your documentation):

     ```
     LoadModule proxy_module modules/mod_proxy.so
     LoadModule proxy_http_module modules/mod_proxy_http.so
     ```
   - Add the following directive to `VirtualHost`:

     ```
     ProxyPreserveHost on
     ```
   - Restart Apache.
2. Use the CherryPy proxy tool as follows:
   - Add the following entry to your global configuration:

     ```
     'tools.proxy.on': True
     ```
   - Restart your CherryPy application.

In both cases, you will now see the following message in your browser:

Hello there http://myapp.com from IP: 127.0.0.1

The IP address stays the same because the test is being done from the same machine where the server is being hosted, on the local interface.

Let's now explain how the previous recipe works. In the first case, by using the `ProxyPreserveHost` directive, we tell Apache to keep the HTTP header host field as it is and not to overwrite it with the local IP address. This means that CherryPy will receive the original value of the Host header.

In the second case, we tell CherryPy to look for specific headers set by Apache when doing proxy with the original hostnames. The default header looked up by CherryPy is `X-Forwarded-Host`.

Lighttpd with mod_proxy Module

Lighttpd is another popular and very efficient HTTP server. The previous section can be translated to lighttpd in a similar fashion using `mod_proxy`. Here is an example on how you can configure lighttpd to proxy incoming requests to a CherryPy server:

```
$HTTP["host"] == "myapp.com"
{
  proxy.server = ( "" => (("host" => "127.0.0.1",
                          "port" => 8080)))
}
```

Add this to the `lighttd.conf` file and restart the server. When browsing to `http://myapp.com`, you will see the following message:

Hello there http://myapp.com from IP: 127.0.0.1

Apache with mod_python Module

In the year 2000, Gregory Trubetskoy released the first version of `mod_python`. It is a module for Apache allowing the Python interpreter to be embedded within the Apache server providing a bridge between the Apache web server and Python applications. One of the strengths of `mod_python` is that unlike CGI where each request requires a Python process to be launched `mod_python` does not have any such requirement. Therefore, it gives the opportunity to the developer to benefit from the persistence of the Python process started by Apache when running the module (keeping a pool of database connections for instance).

Before seeing how to configure Apache and `mod_python`, let's review what are the requirements:

- Apache 2.2
- `mod_python` 3.1.x or superior

We will assume that `mod_python` is properly installed in your environment.

Now let's explain how to configure `mod_python` to run a CherryPy-based application:

```
LoadModule python_module modules/mod_python.so

<Location "/">
  PythonPath "sys.path + ['/home/sylvain/app']"
  SetHandler python-program
  PythonHandler cherrypy._cpmodpy::handler
  PythonOption cherrypy.setup my_app::setup_app
  PythonDebug On
</Location>
```

We will take you through the process sequentially:

1. First we load the `mod_python` module.
2. We define a location directive specifying what Apache should do to the request starting with "/".

3. Then we define several `mod_python` directives:

   ° `PythonPath` extends the system path and makes sure that our application modules will be found. For instance, here the `my_app.py` module resides in `/home/sylvain/app`.

   ° `SetHandler` indicates that all requests starting with the path provided in the location directive will be handled by `mod_python`.

   ° `PythonHandler` sets the generic handler that will be in charge of generating the output to return to the user agent. We use the built-in `mod_python` handler provided by CherryPy.

   ° `PythonOption` passes options to the generic handler. Here the option will be named `cherrypy.setup` and we bind it to the function `setup_app` that our application provides. We assume the application is saved in a Python module named `my_app.py`. The `setup_app` method must be the one mounting the application.

   ° `PythonDebug` is enabled.

4. Finally, we modify the application as follows:

```
import cherrypy

def setup_app():
  class Root:
    @cherrypy.expose
    def index(self):
      return "Hello there %s from IP: %s " % \
      (cherrypy.request.base,cherrypy.request.remote.ip)

  cherrypy.tree.mount(Root())
  cherrypy.engine.start(blocking=False)
```

The difference is that we start the CherryPy engine in a non-blocking mode so that the Python process started via `mod_python` does not hang.

Now you can stop and restart the Apache process and navigate to the `http://myapp.com` URL and you should see the following content:

Hello there http://myapp.com from IP: 127.0.0.1

mod_python with WSGI Application

In the previous approach, we used the built-in mod_python handler that works fine on the applications usually hosted by CherryPy. If your application respects the WSGI interface, you may want to use the ModPythonGateway handler (http://projects.amor.org/misc/wiki/ModPythonGateway) developed by Robert Brewer.

First let's see the CherryPy application in the my_app.py module:

```python
import cherrypy

class Root:
  @cherrypy.expose
  def index(self):
    return "Hello there %s from IP: %s " % (cherrypy.request.base,
    cherrypy.request.remote.ip)

# Create an application respecting the WSGI interface
wsgi_app = cherrypy.Application(Root())

# This will be call on the first request
def setup_app(req):
  cherrypy.engine.start(blocking=False)
```

Now, let's review how to configure Apache to use the ModPythonGateway handler:

```
<Location "/">
  PythonPath "sys.path + ['/home/sylvain/app']"
  SetHandler python-program
  PythonHandler modpython_gateway::handler
  PythonOption wsgi.startup my_app::setup_app
  PythonOption wsgi.application my_app::wsgi_app
  PythonOption wsgi.cleanup cherrypy::engine.stop
</Location>
```

Thanks to the ModPythonGateway handler, you can use the richness of WSGI-based middlewares within the power of the Apache server.

SSL

SSL (**Secure Sockets Layer**) can be supported in CherryPy-based applications natively by CherryPy. To enable SSL support, you must meet the following requirements:

- Have the PyOpenSSL package installed in your environment
- Have an SSL certificate and private key on the server

In the rest of this chapter, we will assume that you have installed PyOpenSSL properly. Let us explain how to generate a pair of private key and certificate. To achieve this, we will use OpenSSL, a common open-source implementation of the SSL specification.

Creating a Certificate and a Private Key

Let's deal with the certificate and the private key:

1. First we need a private key:

   ```
   openssl genrsa -out server.key 2048
   ```

2. This key is not protected by a passphrase and therefore has a fairly weak protection. If you prefer providing a passphrase, you should issue a command like this:

   ```
   openssl genrsa -des3 -out server.key 2048
   ```

   The program will require a passphrase. If your version of OpenSSL allows you to provide an empty string, do so. Otherwise, enter a default passphrase and then remove it from the generated key as follows:

   ```
   openssl rsa -in server.key -out server.key
   ```

3. Now we create a certificate as follows:

   ```
   openssl req -new -key server.key -out server.csr
   ```

4. This process will request you to input some details. The previous step has generated a certificate but it is not yet signed by the private key. To do so, you must issue the following command:

   ```
   openssl x509 -req -days 60 -in server.csr -signkey
                             server.key -out server.crt
   ```

The newly signed certificate will be valid for 60 days.

 Note that, as the certificate is not signed by a recognized authority such as VeriSign, your browser will display a pop up when accessing the application, so that the user can accept or reject the certificate.

Now, we can have a look at the different approaches for creating the certificate and the key.

Using the CherryPy SSL Support

Let's see how we can do it:

```python
import cherrypy
import os, os.path

localDir = os.path.abspath(os.path.dirname(__file__))
CA = os.path.join(localDir, 'server.crt')
KEY = os.path.join(localDir, 'server.key')

def setup_server():
  class Root:
    @cherrypy.expose
    def index(self):
      return "Hello there!"

    cherrypy.tree.mount(Root())
if __name__ == '__main__':
  setup_server()
  cherrypy.config.update({'server.socket_port': 8443,
                          'environment': 'production',
                          'log.screen': True,
                          'server.ssl_certificate': CA,
                          'server.ssl_private_key': KEY})

  cherrypy.server.quickstart()
  cherrypy.engine.start()
```

The key is to provide the `server.ssl_certificate` and `server.ssl_private_key` values to the global CherryPy configuration. The next step is to start the server; if everything went well, you should see the following message on your screen:

HTTP Serving HTTPS on https://localhost:8443/

By navigating to the application URL, you should see a message such as:

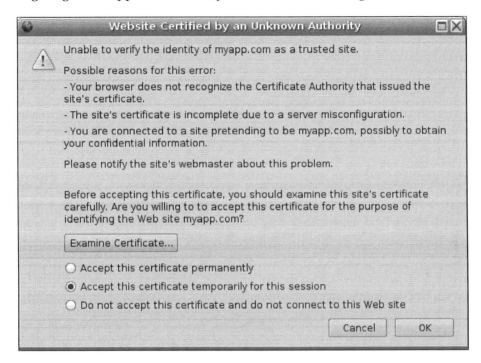

If you accept the certificate, you will be able to continue using the web application via HTTPS.

One caveat of the previous solution is that now your application cannot be reached via non-secured HTTP. Luckily CherryPy provides a fairly easy way to work around this problem by simply starting two HTTP servers at once. You can see how it is done:

```
import cherrypy
from cherrypy import _cpwsgi
from cherrypy import wsgiserver
import os, os.path

localDir = os.path.abspath(os.path.dirname(__file__))
CA = os.path.join(localDir, 'server.crt')
KEY = os.path.join(localDir, 'server.key')

def setup_app():
  class Root:
    @cherrypy.expose
```

```
      def index(self):
         return "Hello there!"

      cherrypy.tree.mount(Root())

   if __name__ == '__main__':
      setup_app()

      # Create a server which will accept HTTP requests
      s1 = _cpwsgi.CPWSGIServer()

      # Create a server which will accept HTTPS requests
      s2 = _cpwsgi.CPWSGIServer()
      s2.ssl_certificate = CA
      s2.ssl_private_key = KEY
      # Our first server uses the default CherryPy settings
      # localhost, 8080. We thus provide distinct ones
      # for the HTTPS server.
      s2.bind_addr = ('localhost', 8443)

      # Inform CherryPy which servers to start and use
      cherrypy.server.httpservers = {s1: ('localhost', 8080),
                                     s2: ('localhost', 8443)}
      cherrypy.server.start()
      cherrypy.engine.start()
```

Upon starting the application, you should now see the following lines on your screen:

HTTP Serving HTTPS on https://localhost:8443/

HTTP Serving HTTP on http://localhost:8080/

Your application will now be reachable via HTTP and HTTPS.

Using the lighttpd SSL Support

Setting SSL support for lighttpd is as simple as adding the following to the global configuration of lighttpd:

```
ssl.engine    = "enable"
ssl.pemfile   = "/home/sylvain/application/server.pem"
```

The `server.pem` file is the concatenation of the `server.key` and `server.crt` files that we have created before. For instance, under a UNIX System we issue the following command:

```
cat server.key server.crt > server.pem
```

By using those two lines and the proxy method, we have described in the previous section how to support SSL for the CherryPy application.

 Note, however, that the path between lighttpd and CherryPy will be HTTP not secured. SSL support will stop at the lighttpd level.

Using the Apache mod_ssl Support

This approach consists of using the `mod_ssl` module of Apache based on OpenSSL to handle the SSL exchange before forwarding the request to the CherryPy server, as we did with lighttpd.

To do so, you need to modify your Apache configuration as follows:

```
LoadModule ssl_module modules/mod_ssl.so

Listen 127.0.0.1:443
```

The first line loads the `mod_ssl` module. The second line requests Apache to listen for incoming socket connections on a given IP address on port 443 (which requires administrator rights).

Then, we modify `VirtualHost`, as follows:

```
<VirtualHost 127.0.0.1:443>
  SSLEngine On
  SSLCertificateFile /home/sylvain/application/server.crt
  SSLCertificateKeyFile /home/sylvain/application/server.key

</VirtualHost>
```

Once you have restarted the Apache process, you should be able to navigate to the URL `https://myapp.com`.

Summary

In this chapter, we have reviewed a few possibilities to configure and deploy the CherryPy-based applications using common products such as Apache and lighttpd. We have also dealt with SSL support. These should give you enough to start with and adapt for your own environment and requirements.

However, deployment goes beyond setting up web servers and this chapter does not cover the discussion of pushing the code into the production environment, neither does it explain how to update the application once in production. This is out of the scope of this chapter and hence not been discussed.

Author's View

If you have read this book, I can only assume that you are interested in the CherryPy library as a candidate for your personal projects. However, my motive behind writing this book was two-fold. Firstly, I wanted to provide a solid reference for CherryPy 3 that could, well hopefully, fill the curiosity of developers using it and this is what I have tried to achieve in the first four chapters of the book.

Secondly, I wished to introduce you, my fellow reader to some of the different aspects of the development of web applications. I did not plan this book as a reference for all the subjects it gets onto, since it would have required ten other tomes. Instead, I have tried to provide you with some of the keys to make you understand that writing a web application is not any different from any other type of application in the process.

With that perspective in mind, Chapter 5 taught us that the persistent mechanism like relational databases could be abstracted, thanks to object-relational mapping like Dejavu, SQLObject, or SQLAlchemy. This is a fundamental concept that allows you to design your application in a relaxed fashion with regards to the manipulated data. Thereafter, Chapter 6 reminded us that a web application could not only serve HTML pages but also expose an API referred to as a web service. This API is precisely what transforms our web application into an actual provider of valuable services. Does it mean we should forget about the actual user experience and be shallow on the designing of the interface of our application? Obviously not, and Chapters 7 and 8 review the idea behind templating before moving to the additional feature of client-side scripting and Ajax. Eventually, Chapter 9 makes sure that we never forget that an application that has not been tested is a broken one, while Chapter 10 provides a few tips to deploy our application in common environments.

I hope this book will tell you a story of web application development that goes beyond CherryPy itself or any of the products introduced. A story that reminds us that there is no right or wrong but some paths that have already been explored might be good and could be trusted and sometimes they should be pushed even further.

As I have said before, I have not written this book as a reference but as an introduction. It is quite possible that you think there are alternatives or better ways to achieve some of the topics covered. In such a case, I would be pleased to discuss this with you on the CherryPy mailing-lists. If on the other hand you close this book and think about parts of its content, then I will reach my goal.

Index

Thank you for buying
CherryPy Essentials

Packt Open Source Project Royalties

When we sell a book written on an Open Source project, we pay a royalty directly to that project. Therefore by purchasing CherryPy Essentials, Packt will have given some of the money received to the CherryPy project.

In the long term, we see ourselves and you—customers and readers of our books—as part of the Open Source ecosystem, providing sustainable revenue for the projects we publish on. Our aim at Packt is to establish publishing royalties as an essential part of the service and support a business model that sustains Open Source.

If you're working with an Open Source project that you would like us to publish on, and subsequently pay royalties to, please get in touch with us.

Writing for Packt

We welcome all inquiries from people who are interested in authoring. Book proposals should be sent to authors@packtpub.com. If your book idea is still at an early stage and you would like to discuss it first before writing a formal book proposal, contact us; one of our commissioning editors will get in touch with you.

We're not just looking for published authors; if you have strong technical skills but no writing experience, our experienced editors can help you develop a writing career, or simply get some additional reward for your expertise.

About Packt Publishing

Packt, pronounced 'packed', published its first book "Mastering phpMyAdmin for Effective MySQL Management" in April 2004 and subsequently continued to specialize in publishing highly focused books on specific technologies and solutions.

Our books and publications share the experiences of your fellow IT professionals in adapting and customizing today's systems, applications, and frameworks. Our solution-based books give you the knowledge and power to customize the software and technologies you're using to get the job done. Packt books are more specific and less general than the IT books you have seen in the past. Our unique business model allows us to bring you more focused information, giving you more of what you need to know, and less of what you don't.

Packt is a modern, yet unique publishing company, which focuses on producing quality, cutting-edge books for communities of developers, administrators, and newbies alike. For more information, please visit our website: www.PacktPub.com.

PUBLISHING

Building Websites with Plone

ISBN: 1-904811-02-7   Paperback: 398 pages

An in-depth and comprehensive guide to the Plone content management system

1. A comprehensive guide for Plone website administrators and developers

2. Design, build, and manage content rich websites using Plone

3. Extend Plone's skins and content types

4. Customize, secure, and optimize Plone websites

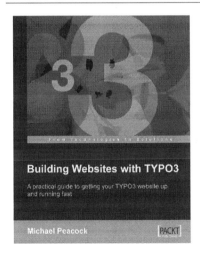

Building Websites with TYPO3

ISBN: 978-1-847191-11-3   Paperback: 250 pages

A practical guide to getting your TYPO3 website up and running fast

1. A practical step-by-step tutorial to creating your TYPO3 website

2. Install and configure TYPO3

3. Master all the important aspects of TYPO3, including the backend, the frontend, content management, and templates

4. Gain hands-on experience by developing an example site through the book

Please visit **www.PacktPub.com** for information on our titles